A LITERARY REVOLUTION

In the Spirit of the Harlem Renaissance

Edited by

Sandra M. Grayson

University Press of America,® Inc.
Lanham · Boulder · New York · Toronto · Plymouth, UK

Copyright © 2008 by
Sandra M. Grayson

University Press of America,® Inc.
4501 Forbes Boulevard
Suite 200
Lanham, Maryland 20706
UPA Acquisitions Department (301) 459-3366

Estover Road
Plymouth PL6 7PY
United Kingdom

Library of Congress Control Number: 2007936540
ISBN-13: 978-0-7618-3924-8 (paperback : alk. paper)
ISBN-10: 0-7618-3924-0 (paperback : alk. paper)

♾™ The paper used in this publication meets the minimum
requirements of American National Standard for Information
Sciences—Permanence of Paper for Printed Library Materials,
ANSI Z39.48—1984

To Jimmie R. Grayson, Jr., Ssanyu Makeda Grayson, and
Suru Mayokun Grayson

Contents

Philosophy

Foreword

A Literary Revolution: In the Spirit of the Harlem Renaissance is a remarkable and important anthology. Sandra M. Grayson has collected and organized a range of literary works that reflect the comprehensive and complex set of social, class, and political experiences encompassed by what is known as the "African Diaspora." Grayson also has provided space for writers and activists to share their insights about the myriad challenges faced by those interested in expanding democracy in Africa and in the international arena.

This anthology serves to remind us about the earlier and ongoing linkages of people of African descent, including African Americans, throughout the international arena. This is a special strength of the anthology and one that is bolted enormously with the insights and work of the editor. Very importantly, and in a creative manner, Sandra M. Grayson includes the voices of people directly involved with struggles for social change. These featured voices are scholars and activists in the fields of literature, politics, government, philosophy, the arts, and film. Grayson also utilizes interviews with prominent individuals to highlight issues like gender, intellectual responsibility to society, class, national consciousness, and collective memory.

This book makes a major contribution to African Studies and African American Studies, as well as to connecting the varied experiences of African Americans with the insights and thoughts of African thinkers and writers. In a very powerful way, we hear the thoughts of African intellectuals regarding the varied experiences faced by black people in the United States. Thus, the title of this anthology, *A Literary Revolution: In the Spirit of the Harlem Renaissance*, is quite apt in that it will serve to

re-ignite the thirst and need for people of African descent to communicate with each other about their collective experiences.

James Jennings
Tufts University

Preface

Sandra M. Grayson

A Literary Revolution: In the Spirit of the Harlem Renaissance recalls a primary goal of black movements that have advocated that people of African descent speak for and represent themselves. One such example can been seen through the *Colored American Magazine* (established in 1900 and published in Boston). Hazel Carby observes, "The staff of the *Colored American Magazine* [including Pauline Hopkins, an editorial force for the magazine from 1900-1904 and an author] considered their journal to be a tool in the creation of a black renaissance, an inspiration for 'Theologians, Artists, [and] Scientists' whose theories had grown dormant for lack of a channel of communication" (163).

In the 1920s, a black renaissance emerged that Sterling Brown described as a literary, art, and music movement with "temporal roots in the past and spatial roots elsewhere in America" (57-58). The Harlem Renaissance can be seen as a continuing tradition of artistic revolution, and the "spirit" of the movement as an enterprise of networking in black communities. Jessie Fauset, one of the black writers and patrons of this movement, exemplifies its significance. She, like other leaders of the movement including W.E.B. DuBois and Alain Locke, regarded fiction and art as means to achieve social change.

A Literary Revolution: In the Spirit of the Harlem Renaissance reinforces one of the primary goals of the aforementioned black renaissances—that people of African descent represent themselves. Original works, diverse perspectives, varied voices, and multiple disciplines intersect in this book to analyze the complexities of the selected subjects.

Milwaukee, Wisconsin
August, 2007

Works Cited

Brown, Sterling. "The New Negro in Literature 1925-1955." *The New Negro Thirty Years Afterward*, papers contributed to the Sixteenth Annual Spring Conference of the Division of Social Science, Howard University Graduate School. Washington, D.C. Ed. Rayford W. Logan, et al. Washington: Howard University Press, 1955. 57-72.

Carby, Hazel V. *Reconstructing Womanhood: The Emergence of the Afro-American Woman Novelist*. New York: Oxford University Press, 1987.

Introduction

Sandra M. Grayson

Featuring a wide range of perspectives of people of African descent, *A Literary Revolution: In the Spirit of the Harlem Renaissance* brings together groundbreaking essays, interviews, short stories, and poems to explore a mosaic of experiences of black people. The "spirit" of the Harlem Renaissance was one of networking in black communities and in that spirit this book was created. Original works, diverse views, and multiple disciplines intersect in *A Literary Revolution*. The primary goals are to examine significant issues that are overlooked or that have not yet been fully explored; to provide original analyses of the selected subjects; and to present innovative creative writing.

Through its methodology and scope, *A Literary Revolution* begins to address what Cornel West describes as the "modern Black diaspora problematic of invisibility and namelessness," which he argues "can be understood as the condition of *relative lack of Black power to represent themselves to themselves and others as complex human beings, and thereby to contest the bombardment of negative, degrading stereotypes put forward by White supremacist ideologies*" (27). In *A Literary Revolution*, people of African descent speak for and represent themselves. Voices range from a member of the African National Congress to award-winning writers; internationally recognized professors to new scholars; philosophers in Nigeria to activists in South Africa.

The works utilize diverse methodologies to explore the complexities of the selected subjects and to provide insights into selected literatures, histories, traditional beliefs, cultures, experiences, and worldviews of people of African descent. Divided into four parts (South Africa; Literature and Film; Short Stories and Poetry; and Philosophy), *A Literary Revolution* reflects a tapestry of experiences of black people.

Through autobiographical narrative, essays, poetry, and an interview, the first part of this book explores experiences of black people in South Africa. "From Azania and Back: Reflections on Exile" details the challenges that Alosi J. M. Moloi faced in South Africa during apartheid and his subsequent exile—first in Botswana then in the United States. In 1963, Moloi left South Africa for Botswana, where he had a different frame of reference from that in South Africa. He retuned to South Africa in 1966. However, realizing that South Africa was no longer safe for him or his family, he relocated to the United States, where he began his second phase of exile.

"An Interview with Lavinia Africa" by Sandra M. Grayson and Muyiwa Falaiye focuses on Lavinia Africa's social activism and political poems. Africa, a poet and member of the African National Congress (ANC), formerly taught at the University of the Western Cape in South Africa. On the eve of the Tricameral Parliament elections in South Africa (21 August 1984), she was a student activist and member of the United Democratic Front (UDF). In Ravensmead, a small town in the Northern Suburbs of Cape Town, South Africa, a protest march was arranged for that date. She was among the 200 protesters who were chased by thousands of police. She could not get away in time, and the white police officers severely beat her. The police used batons to beat the protesters until they were unconscious or dead. Her poem "Baton Charged" represents the 1984 protest march in Ravensmead that was disrupted by thousands of white police officers who used batons to beat the unarmed protesters.

The award-winning poet Chimalum Nwankwo pays tribute to Xhamela, Walter Sisulu (18 May 1912 - 5 May 2003), in "Walking into the Sea." Sisulu was a former South African liberation leader, civil-rights activist, deputy president of the ANC, and mentor to numerous South Africans (including former South African president Nelson Mandela). Mandela described Sisulu as one of the greatest freedom fighters ("Former ANC Leader . . ."). President Thabo Mbeki explained that Sisulu, one of the major architects of the ANC, played a central role as one of the primary leaders and activists of the movement for 60 years ("Letter from the President"). In "Politics of Multilingualism in South Africa," Alosi J. M. Moloi argues that African languages and traditions in South Africa/Azania must not be forsaken for English language and culture. He explores ways to combat the trend of marginalizing African languages.

"Reunion at the Jazz Castle" by Patric Tariq Mellet is a tribute to Mervyn Africa, one of South Africa's finest Jazz pianists. The poem was inspired by Africa's reunion performance in South Africa. In August 2000, he returned to South Africa after over twenty years in exile in the United Kingdom. Ronald Dorris in "Voice in the New South Africa" discusses his experience in the United States/South Africa National Cultural Heritage and Technology Training program, a three-year project. He spent six weeks in South Africa during summer 2002. He focuses on the question of *voice* in the new South Africa juxtaposed with Jean Toomer's philosophy. In "Engineering Patriotism: Americanization and Afrikanerization," Patrick Rankhumise analyzes parallels between Americanization in North America and Afrikanerization in South Africa. Prince Mbusi Dube in "Economic Aspects of Historical African Art" discusses ways to analyze traditional African art, with emphasis on works created in South Africa. He also explores several economic elements of traditional African art.

The filmmakers and writers of focus include Julie Dash, Pauline Hopkins, Akachi Adimora-Ezeigbo, Haile Gerima, and Jean Toomer. In "Screen *Jelimuso*: Julie Dash and Political Films," Sandra M. Grayson focuses on the award-winning black independent filmmaker Julie Dash and analyzes two of Dash's films (*The Rosa Parks Story* and *Daughters of the Dust*) as political films. Grayson uses the phrase *screen jelimuso* to describe a black woman independent filmmaker who is concerned with preserving and presenting history and who has artistic status. As a messenger and visionary, a *screen jelimuso* poses critical alternatives to mainstream cinema, uses film as both a political tool and artistic medium, as well as continues and transforms the African American oral tradition. In "Recalling Sovereign Kentakes: Pauline Hopkins' *Of One Blood*," Sandra M. Grayson analyzes the images of black women in the novel that are linked (through direct reference or symbolism) to female rulers of ancient African nations. *Of One Blood* represents *mythic spaces* where the seemingly impossible is possible and where alternative ways of representing and knowing the world are explored.

In a thought-provoking interview, Akachi Adimora-Ezeigbo discusses her works in context and details some of her experiences in Nigeria. Internationally recognized in the literary world and the academy, Adimora-Ezeigbo is a novelist, Professor, and former Chair of the English Department at the University of Lagos in Nigeria. In "Pauline Hopkins and Social Justice," Joy Myree-Mainor analyzes *Contending Forces* in the context of Hopkins' social and political activism. The novel, she argues, challenges racist ideologies. Myree-Mainor observes, "Hopkins remained a forerunner in promoting the need to uncover the systematic nature of racism."

Samuel Ayedime Kafewo in "Trans-Atlantic Dimensions: Exploring *Amistad* and *Sankofa*" examines the representation of the slave experience in the two selected films. He describes *Amistad* as "an *assimilation story* that celebrates and glorifies white men, many of whom were slaveholders." Kafewo argues that *Sankofa* is a *resistance story*, where "the enslaved Africans are represented as complex individuals who tell their own stories." *Sankofa* represents the ways that the enslaved resisted slavery and fought for their freedom. "Jean Toomer's 'Kabnis': Family Portrait as Face of the South" by Ronald Dorris explores Toomer's work juxtaposed with Toomer's family history and unveils the multidimensional meanings in "Kabnis" from *Cane*. Through archival research, Dorris decodes the meaning of characters in the context of Toomer's word-game associations, creating names to suit the person, occasion, and mood. Angles of analysis include "the contest between Bis and his father, Pinchback" and symbols associated with "periodic unsteadiness that governed the Pinchback household."

The selected short stories and poems present innovative, complex representations. Inspired by the Ifa Literary Corpus[1] and set in a mythical ancient African empire located west of Lake Chad near modern-day Nigeria, Sandra M. Grayson's story "Transfiguration" focuses on Ase (a woman whose name means "power" in the Yoruba language and who can change forms), the government's reaction to her, and Ase's impact on the nation. Powerful metaphors and complex imagery accentuate Chimalum Nwankwo's tribute to Funmilayo Ransome-Kuti in "Silent Steps." Ransome-Kuti (1900-1978) organized a series of protests (including tax strikes) against British colonial rule. She "participated actively in pre-independence talks in London and subsequently played a leading role in western Nigerian politics and women's mobilization" (Kolawole 49). Using effective imagery, "Pain" by Bose Ademilua-Afolayan shows the depth of the narrator's emotion. "Can You Hook a Brother Up?" by John C. Gaston captures a moment between friends as they recall a former classmate. Through ideal rhythm and precise detail, the poem reflects the varied directions life can take people from the same neighborhood. Ronald Dorris' stories "Dilla" and "Queen Etouffée" bring to life narratives that recall African folktales. Dorris' two poems "Rip Tide" and "Will Mamadou Serve as Guide" were inspired in Dakar,

Senegal. Rich in imagery, the poems effectively symbolize sorrow and hope, separation and connection.

Essays by Muyiwa Falaiye, Friday Nwankwo Ndubuisi, and Ayo Fadahunsi explore the discipline of philosophy in the context of African cultures. Muyiwa Falaiye begins his essay ("Who's Afraid of African Philosophy?") by analyzing three main ways African philosophy has been defined. He observes, "African philosophy refers to the fundamental and general principles governing the community of people called Africans," and philosophy is a conscious discipline that requires analyzing and logically arranging beliefs in a valid and rational way. Falaiye argues, "African philosophy, and by extension cultural philosophy, will help promote integration and world peace."

Friday Nwankwo Ndubuisi in "The Science of African Epistemology" examines the features of African epistemology. He observes that it is essential that research focusing on Africa includes an accurate "understanding of and appreciation for African theories of knowledge." In "African Traditional Medicine: The Metaphysical Foundation," Ndubuisi explores the originality and ingenuity of African traditional medicine, which he describes as holistic. He argues, "Traditional Africans identified *spirit* as the ultimate working principle," and "the practice of medicine in traditional Africa is spiritual. Africans trace ailments beyond the physical."

Ayo Fadahunsi in "Yoruba Names and Meanings: A Metaphysical Interpretation" explores the connection between an individual's name and her/his destiny in the context of Yoruba society in Nigeria. "In traditional Yoruba philosophy," he says, "an individual and her/his destiny are two inseparable factors." He explains that *oruko* (name) is a linguistic symbol, not a mark or branding and that "the metaphysics of names is connected to the unseen reality of these names. This means that names go beyond the objective physicality they represent."

A Literary Revolution: In the Spirit of the Harlem Renaissance recalls the primary objective of some 19th and early 20th century black editors and authors (including Samuel E. Cornish, John B. Russwurm, Anna Julia Cooper, and Pauline Hopkins)—that black people record and represent the experiences of people of African descent. In the first volume (16 March 1827) of *Freedom's Journal*, the editors Samuel E. Cornish and John B. Russwurm explain that black people want to speak for themselves.[2] They add, "Too long have others spoken for us. Too long has the publick been deceived by misrepresentations, in things which concern us dearly. . . . From the press and the pulpit we have suffered much by being incorrectly represented" (1). Anna Julia Cooper[3] in *A Voice from the*

South (1892) issues a call for black people to represent people of African descent from the standpoint of black people (225). Similarly, Pauline Hopkins[4] argued that black people must be responsible for accurately representing the experiences of people of African descent, and she regarded writing (in this case fiction) as a means to achieve social change.[5] *A Literary Revolution* suggests that to begin to decolonize the mind requires (re)visioning the future, questioning the present, and creating profoundly new visions of history.

Notes

1. Wande Abimbola in *Sixteen Great Poems of Ifa* observes that the Ifa Literary Corpus represents the traditional Yoruba worldview and is "the storehouse of Yoruba culture inside which the Yoruba comprehension of their own historical experiences and understanding of their environment can always be found. Even until today Ifa is recognized by the Yoruba as a repository for Yoruba traditional body of knowledge embracing history, philosophy, medicine and folklore" (32).

2. *Freedom's Journal*, the first black owned and operated newspaper published in North America, featured international, national, and regional information on many subjects, including everything that relates to Africa in order to provide accurate information about "that vast continent" (Cornish and Russwurum 1).

3. Anna Julia Cooper was "a leading black spokeswoman of her time" and a leader in women's organizations whose "work in educating black students spanned nearly half a century" (Washington xxvii). "She was one of three black women invited to address the World's Congress of Representative Women in 1893 and one of the few women to speak at the 1900 Pan-African Congress Conference in London" (Washington xxvii). Louise Daniel Hutchinson observes:

> [I]mportant work was done at this meeting, which resulted in the drafting of one of the earliest documents by Africans and people of African descent to address the issue of apartheid in South Africa. According to Owen Charles Mathurin (*Henry Sylvester Williams and the Origins of the Pan-African Movement, 1869-1911*), the Pan-African Conference of 1900 was called to: (1) Establish closer communication among people of African descent scattered around the world, as a result of slavery. (2) To develop plans that would promote more friendly relations between whites and blacks. And, (3) To start a movement that would result in the recognition of full citizenship rights for all Africans and their descendents living in civilized countries, and "to promote their business interest." (111-112)

4. Pauline Hopkins (1859-1930) published extensively in a wide range of gen-
    res. She was also an editorial force (1900-1904) for the *Colored American
    Magazine*. Her publications include the novel *Contending Forces* (1900),
    three magazine novels published serially between March 1901 and Novem-
    ber 1903 (*Hagar's Daughter: A Story of Southern Caste Prejudice*; *Winona:
    A Tale of Negro Life in the South and Southwest*; and *Of One Blood: Or, The
    Hidden Self*), the novella *Topsy Turvey* (1916), short stories, essays, the non-
    fiction work *A Primer of Facts Pertaining to the Early Greatness of the Afri-
    can Race and the Possibility of Restoration by its Descendents* (1905), and
    the musical dramas *Colored Aristocracy* (1877) and *Slave's Escape: or the
    Underground Railroad* (1879). Published in 1900, Hopkins' "The Mystery
    Within Us" is the first speculative fiction short story by a black woman.
5. In the introduction to *The Magazine Novels of Pauline Hopkins*, Hazel Carby
    explains, "Fiction, Hopkins thought, could reach the many classes of citizen
    who never read history or biography, and thus she created fictional histories
    with a pedagogic function: narratives of the relations between the races that
    challenged racist ideologies" (xxxv).

Works Cited

Carby, Hazel V. Introduction. *The Magazine Novels of Pauline Hopkins*. New
York: Oxford University Press, 1988. 441-621.

Cooper, Anna Julia. *A Voice From the South*. 1892. New York: Oxford University Press, 1988.

Cornish, Samuel E. and John B. Russwurm. "To Our Patrons." *Freedom's Journal* 1.1 (16 March 1827): 1.

"Former ANC Leader Walter Sisulu Laid to Rest." *Africa Online* (19 May
2003). http://www.africaonline.com/site/Articles/1,3,53018.jsp

Hopkins, Pauline. Preface. *Contending Forces*. By Pauline Hopkins. 1899. New
York: Oxford University Press, 1988. 13-16.

Hutchinson, Louise Daniel. *Anna J. Cooper, A Voice from the South*. Washington: Smithsonian Institution Press, 1981.

Kolawole, Mary E. Modupe. *Womanism and African Consciousness*. New Jersey: Africa World Press, 1997.

Mbeki, Thabo. "Letter from the President." *ANC Today* 3.19 (16-22 May 2003).
http://www.anc.org.za/ancdocs/anctoday/2003/at19.htm#preslet

"Nation Bids Farewell to Sisulu, 'Quiet Giant' of the Struggle." *allAfrica.com*
(17 May 2003). http://allafrica.com/stories/200305170020.html

"Nelson Mandela's Tribute to Walter Sisulu." *BBC News Online* (6 May 2003).
http://news.bbc.co.uk/2/hi/africa/3003849.stm

Washington, Mary Helen. Introduction. *A Voice From the South*. By Anna Julia
Cooper. New York: Oxford University Press, 1988. xxvii-liv.

West, Cornel. "The New Cultural Politics of Difference." *Out There: Marginalization and Contemporary Cultures.* Eds. Russell Ferguson, Martha Gever, and Trinh T. Minh-ha. New York: Museum of Contemporary Art, 1990. 19-36.

South Africa

1

From Azania and Back:
Reflections on Exile

Alosi J. M. Moloi

In March 1963, I left South Africa for Moeng College in Botswana, leaving a permanent teaching position at Orlando West Secondary School in Johannesburg, South Africa. I only had fifty rands (about seventy five U.S. dollars then) in my pocket since I had not received any pay from the Department of Bantu Education since I began teaching in January 1962, first at Bethel Teacher Training College in the Western Transvaal and then Orlando West High School. Paying African teachers on time, especially new ones, was not a priority with that racialist department. The local school boards, usually headed by incompetent high school level, white fearing church leaders, did not make any serious effort to resolve pay problems for teachers. Thus teachers, highly stressed out, had to borrow money from family and friends even to raise train fare to Pretoria to inquire about their overdue pay, only to be met by haughty low achieving white female clerks who rudely demanded to know why one didn't wait until the department found time to process pay paperwork that was over twelve months overdue.

I got fed up with the daily humiliations of the apartheid system, and I began to hate white people in South Africa intensely, not because they were white, but because of what they had made me become, an angry young man who wanted to destroy the evil system that humiliated my people daily because of their color. I was preparing to get married, and my fiancée, Esther Ntombini Mofokeng, and I had long decided we were not going to take it any more. We were not going to raise our children in a hostile, evil environment dominated by neo-Hitlerites. A school teacher by profession, Esther earned only twenty five rands a month which she too had not received since beginning her teaching career in January 1962.

Leaving South Africa was not easy as the apartheid regime would not grant passports to Africans except permanent exit papers that forbade the user to return to South Africa, or a brown travel document that permitted limited travel to Botswana, Swaziland, and Lesotho, normally valid for three months from date of issue. I opted for the latter document which was already stamped: "Valid for three months from date of issue." The problem was that it had already expired when Moeng College offered me a teaching position which I accepted, and I planned to leave right away. I took a chance buying a second class coach one-way ticket to Palapye, Botswana. I hoped I would find an incompetent Afrikaner immigration officer who did not understand English and confuse him about the meaning of "Valid for three months from date of issue." I was desperate to cross to Botswana.

At Ramatlabama, a border post siding on the border of Botswana and South Africa with no rail platform, Africans were to get off the train with their luggage for passport control. Afrikaner immigration officers took turns to humiliate African passengers while the white passengers, whose passports were checked at Mafeking inside the train, were left undisturbed in their train compartments. Often the African passengers had to chase after the moving train with their luggage whenever it was time to leave Ramatlabama. I got off the train with hundreds of other African passengers. Trying to look as humble and as intimidated as possible, I approached a portly built old Afrikaner officer. In deliberately broken Afrikaans, I requested he stamp my papers. At first, he seemed to understand the words "Valid for three months from date of issue," and he was about to order a black police man to escort me to the "violators" section (those who attempted to leave South Africa without valid documents). Several other unfortunate Africans had already been bundled up in that section awaiting an uncertain future, perhaps torture and imprisonment, or mysterious disappearance in police custody. I feared for my safety as I quickly explained: "Sir, the officer at the Bantu Affairs Commissioner's office assured me that my papers would be valid only on the day I left

South Africa. I want to leave today and be back before the three months expire."

I wanted to appear and sound as illiterate as possible as I pretended not to know what "Valid for three months from date of issue" meant. The Afrikaner's ego was boosted; however, he seemed to doubt his own understanding of English as he examined my travel document again. Then he cursed those clerks at the Commissioner's office, stamped my papers, and sternly admonished me to return to South Africa before the stipulated period in that document. Slightly relieved, I hurried back to my compartment thanking my lucky stars. "Botswana, here I come," I thought to myself even though I did not know what awaited me in that country.

With other Africans, I boarded the segregated train carriage for Africans which was hooked directly to the engine. The whites occupied the rest of the train running between Johannesburg and Bulawayo, formerly Rhodesia. After all, both South Africa and Southern Rhodesia practiced racial segregation. Yet the dining car was "integrated" once the train crossed into Botswana. Some courageous Africans ventured into that part of the train while the majority preferred the relative safety of their allotted compartments holding six passengers each. Once on Botswana territory, I entered the dining car and ordered my meal and a glass of wine. Some racialists voiced their disapproval, rudely staring and cursing at a handful of Africans among them. Some teenagers came to my table and deliberately spilled my glass of wine in full view of the train waiter who was also white. I was furious, and in a rage, I bellowed: "Punks, this is not South Africa. I will gladly kill you as I also loathe the likes of you and apartheid. Your days are numbered." There was absolute silence around me, perhaps out of fear, or perhaps shock as most whites in South Africa were not used to Africans confronting them fearlessly as I did at that moment. Everyone turned to his or her own plate; the waiter refilled my glass; the teenagers scurried to their table, and I calmly proceeded to sample my meal. My fellow Africans had hurriedly devoured their meals, some leaving their beer unfinished at the table. I did not blame them for I knew the reign of terror in South Africa that had cowed down so many of our people. After all, in South Africa, we were totally segregated from each other in separate schools, neighborhoods, and destinies. The whites ruled, abused, oppressed, and humiliated us, while we, the dispossessed Africans, suffered police brutality, utter poverty, terror and untold pain. For that, I hated the racialists in my country.

Living in Botswana provided me with a new frame of reference quite different from that in South Africa. Batswana, who were also under the

English, did not experience debilitating segregation and racial hatred as in South Africa. Whites were clustered around the railway sidings for the most part, leaving Batswana in their villages, and having limited contact with them in their households as servants or in the colonial offices. Batswana were more certain of their African traditional institutions, confident of a better tomorrow as they were on the verge of independence. In fact, their elite were now involved in Responsible Government Institutions. Kgosi Seretse Khama, who had been banished in Britain for several years for marrying a white woman, was back in Botswana where he later led his country to independence. The people were Africans, through and through Batswana! Something that had been taken away from South Africans. Of course, the new elite were aspiring to be white. Some of them spoke only English in their homes, changing their children into black Englishmen. The new tool of destruction of traditional values was, ironically, the English medium school. Yet this environment was different from South Africa. People showed a genuine respect for one another. There was little fear and no police or security force terror. There was some openness in human relations, with some black and white people forming genuine friendships and relationships. American Peace Corps and British Voluntary Service Organization volunteers added to the population mix of Botswana, although some of those volunteers believed they were in Africa to save black people from themselves. In general, people related to one another as human beings in Botswana, not as master and servant.

South Africa, on the other hand, had been a different story where the population was seriously fragmented. Asians were Asians, Whites were Whites, Coloreds were Coloreds, and Africans were by themselves, with the racialist regime working diligently to fragment us further according to language spoken. We knew nothing about one another, except that we distrusted, envied, or even hated one another. Apartheid fed on fear, suspicion, envy, and ruthless competition among ethnic groups. Botswana intensified my hatred for apartheid and my determination to work for the destruction of that evil system. Knowing better alternatives to apartheid, sensing spurious claims of white supremacy myths, and having tasted some freedom and semblance of justice, I was not prepared to allow foreigners to decimate us in the land of our birth.

In Palapye and Serowe, I joined the first wave of exiles from both South West Africa and South Africa who had left in the mid-fifties and early sixties. There were those who were marked for death by the racialist regime because they were known liberation movement leaders, others were in danger because of their association with the former group, while others still were not affiliated to any other political organization even though they also hated the regime and oppression they had left behind. There were also economic refugees who wanted to escape the cruelty in South West Africa and South Africa. Whatever the reasons for exile, we were all the victims of apartheid terrorism. Most kept to themselves, not trusting anyone, not knowing who was friend or foe. After all, South African agents were operating openly in Botswana. There were night raids, kidnapings, and murder which the ineffectual and timid Botswana police could not stop. Fear and suspicions in the exile community were understandable. The then Colonial Administrators in Botswana were collaborating and cooperating with South Africa. For example, some exiles were expelled from Botswana for no apparent reason. My friend Mrs. Kerina was forced off her teaching position at Moeng College because of her husband's struggles against illegal South African occupation of South West Africa. In fact, the colonialists made life difficult for South African exiles in Botswana.

However, Botswana was also an eye opener to the scope of the liberation struggle in South Africa. Some European expatriates, as well as most Batswana, could not understand how a small minority of whites in South Africa could oppress and control such a large African population. They wondered, "Why couldn't we take up arms and drive the oppressors into the sea?" "Was it because the whites were superior to Africans as they have often alleged?" Heated arguments ensued at the pubs or wherever the people aggregated to account for European racism, international governments, and multi-national companies' involvement in South Africa. South Africans argued passionately how we were fighting far more serious external forces than the settler oppressors in our country. Apartheid apologists, on the other hand, bemoaned the failure of independent African states, listing them as the major factor hardening the hearts of whites in South Africa. They urged caution and patience, imploring Africans to give whites time to come around. Sometimes that argument was presented out of ignorance, while at times it was from haughtiness and contempt for Africans. Whatever the reason, at least in Botswana we talked about South Africa, analyzed the situation, reflected, and offered suggestions for change in that troubled country. We had the opportunity to see the problem from outside, at a distance, and realized its urgency.

Another group of South African exiles I interacted with was the "Rhodesia" exile community that fought a similarly racialist regime in their country. They became our natural allies while our hosts, Batswana elite, kept to themselves. They were fewer in number relative to the population of their country, allying themselves with the neo-royalists whose status derived from traditional institutions. To them, we were "Matla-le-seporo" those who came along the railway line, outsiders with no status in Botswana. Although we were the teachers in their schools, nurses and doctors in their hospitals, professionals in various capacities, we were the guests who had overstayed their welcome. Batswana were aloof.

However, after gaining independence in 1966, Kgosi Khama's government pledged support for the liberation of South Africa and worked with Zambia and Tanzania to improve the condition of the victims of apartheid. Conditions for South African exiles in Botswana improved, except that those former South Africans who had taken Botswana citizenship were very vicious and oppressive towards other South Africans. Those in the ministries controlling education and immigration, especially, were insensitive to the needs of their former compatriots. Probably this is the problem with "paper citizens" (naturalized citizens); they become more citizens than those actually born in that country. In Zambia too, those South Africans who had become Zambians tended to abuse their authority against exiles.

My first phase of exile in Botswana was a learning experience, as well as a training session for Botswana. We educated young Batswana who became the first officials of the newly independent state of Botswana. It was gratifying to see former students become ambassadors, assistant attorney generals, school inspectors, immigration officers, and other government officials. This is what we also envisaged for an independent South Africa, free of white domination and racial discrimination. If Botswana and other African countries gained their independence, what would stop us, South Africans, from realizing that goal? Botswana kept our dreams, hopes, aspirations, and yearning for freedom alive. Knowing what a better alternative freedom was to the inhumane neo-Nazi apartheid system, encouraged those of us who had tasted some liberty outside South Africa to resist in earnest and encourage our compatriots to overthrow the evil system in our country. Long before the U.N. General Assembly declared it, we knew that apartheid was a crime against humanity, and therefore, since it could not be reformed, it was to be utterly smashed. It was with that spirit that I returned to South Africa to accept a lectureship at the University of the North in Pietersburg in 1966.

I was under the watchful eyes of the stewards of apartheid for having dared to leave the country before and speak my mind. Even our timid

African brothers in high positions at Turfloop (the nickname of the University of the North) and those at Unisa, Pretoria would caution me to "tow the line." I would constantly be admonished that: "Moloi, Jy ry jou perd te vinnig" (Moloi, you are riding your horse too fast. Beware it will throw you off). I understood their concern, although I despised their cowardice and timidity since they were willing to accept humiliation and oppression as long as they continued to receive crumbs from their masters' tables. As long as they were out of their masters' way and causing no problems, these timid men were content. They hated political activists like myself, whom they labeled "trouble makers." The truth is, no one who had seen the light, especially from outside South Africa, would let sleeping dogs lie and endure the despotic, unnatural, and evil government of apartheid.

The next three years in South Africa were difficult with callous and brutal abuse meted out on political activists, especially the students. However, the students were brave; they continued to organize, mobilize, educate one another and the surrounding communities. Progress was slow, but it was encouraging. I was privileged to enjoy the trust of the members of the South African Student Organization (SASO) who often invited me to address them on a range of topics covering the evils of apartheid, political treachery of Bantustans, liberations movements, and resistance to national enslavement. Watching the courage of young students in the face of the callous and cruel oppressors strengthened us and raised our hopes for collective struggle to overturn the enemy. I believe hope also reached the operatives of the evil regime because, instead of arresting me or known students activists, African policemen, reputed to fear the boers, would secretly come to my home to warn me of impending danger or plots to trap us. They admitted their timidity and helplessness, yet they believed saving some of the opponents of apartheid from incarceration was their small contribution to the liberation struggle. Their concern kept me out of jail and terror of South African security forces, or as the people called them, Satan After People forces (S.A.P.)

The university authorities did not trust me as it became evident in 1969 when I was offered a Fulbright grant to the United States. I was diligently advised to watch what I did and said abroad because the university and the government had means of knowing every movement I made. The university administrators never hid the fact that they were government agents more than they were academicians. They were thus used to intimidating defenseless Africans, except that they had miscalculated dealing with this particular African, ME.

My United States hosts afforded me the greatest opportunity to tour and lecture in several cities and states. Many could not believe the details of the evil system I was describing to them. Community organizations and student audiences gave me strength, and fearlessly I spoke about our struggle right up to the United Nations where I conducted a Winter seminar for Bethany College students. The more I gave interviews and exchanged views with various organizations and individuals, the more I knew I could no longer operate safely in South Africa. I feared for my own safety, my family's, and my students'. I had to get out, or certainly I would have gone to prison, for the regime hated Africans who struggled against oppression. Six months later, I returned from my U.S. trip, finding my employers agitated and infuriated by my lectures and interviews during my absence. They had kept their word, keeping track of my every movement. I also made matters worse by addressing SASO and other groups on our struggle and its legitimacy. For example, one evening SASO branch at Turfloop invited me to address the group on the historical development of Bantustans, a topic tracing European treachery to dispossess Africans and leave them a poverty-stricken, landless proletariat crowded on barren, desolate, rural slums. Government spies also attended, reporting their anger to the rector of the university. The next morning the rector, his registrar, and other white officials, summoned me to his office demanding that I turn over a copy of my paper and accusing me of being an enemy of South Africa who was instigating students against the authority of the State. I vehemently resisted, defending academic freedom and the students' rights to hear lectures on any topic about South Africa. Finally, I handed over the copy of my speech to the university authorities-turned-government agents, and in protest I handed in my resignation. South Africa was no longer safe for me, and I had to leave the country before something bad happened to me. My previous trip to the United States as a Fulbright Scholar paid off as my contacts were able to introduce me to University of California, Los Angeles, which offered me a teaching position in the Department of Linguistics and association with their dynamic and progressive African Studies Center. A new chapter in my life began, and a new frame of reference developed in my second phase of exile.

2

An Interview with Lavinia Africa

Sandra M. Grayson and Muyiwa Falaiye

GRAYSON and FALAIYE: Your poem "Baton Charged" is based on a protest march in a town in the Northern Suburbs of Cape Town, South Africa. What details can you provide about that event and your participation in the protest?[1]

AFRICA: The protest march took place on the eve of 24 August 1984 when the Tricameral Parliament was launched in South Africa. The Tricameral Parliament included Whites, Coloureds (a term used by the government to refer to several groups of people, including principally those whom they deem to be of descent that is mixed in terms of the categories of apartheid), and Indians (constituting the great majority of those officially termed Asian). The Tricameral Parliament excluded Africans (the majority of the black community which was denied participation in central government and was assigned to the Bantustan system). The local MP (Member of Parliament) of Ravensmead, an area in the Northern Suburbs of Cape Town, held a mass meeting by invitation only. Comrades and their families were excluded from attending the meeting where various important issues affecting the community would have been discussed. We decided to protest outside the Civic Center by toy-toying[2] and singing freedom songs. Police were called in, and we were given two minutes to disperse. The first teargas canister was shot into the crowd, and we started to run down the streets, facing police in camouflaged clothes. We had to re-route into the yards and into the houses. At this point, I found myself knocking on the door of one of the houses, and they would not open the door. I jumped over the fence and found myself in another yard hiding behind the dog kennel with two other comrades. The dog barked continuously and attracted police attention. A few minutes later we heard police voices, and a torch was shining on us. We were caught. The police started beating us, and we tried to run away. After passing about ten policemen who aimed for my head, I fainted. After a few seconds, I gained consciousness, lying down on my left side covering my head with my right arm. About 30 policemen continued beating me. I realized I had to get away because the beatings wouldn't stop. I got up, weak in my legs, ran down the road to the nearest house while still being chased and beaten. People shouted at the police to stop the beating and to leave me alone. Eventually, when I entered the yard they stopped and turned back. The occupants of the house brought warm water and clothes to try and stop the bleeding. They arranged a car and rushed me to the nearest hospital, Tygerberg Hospital.

GRAYSON and FALAIYE: Please discuss some of the themes in your other poems.

AFRICA: Some of the themes in my other poems include family and activism. Examples can be seen in my poems "Thabo Nelson Africa" and "On the Run."[3] The poem "Thabo Nelson Africa" is about the name of my son. His first name is Thabo named after Thabo Mbeki, the current President of South Africa. At the time of my son's birth Thabo Mbeki was in exile, and we as parents thought Thabo would be the first democratically elected president of South Africa after apartheid. "Nelson" is his middle name, after Nelson Mandela (Madiba) because he was born on Mandela's birthday, 18 July. At the time of my son's birth, Nelson Mandela was serving a life sentence as a political prisoner on Robben Island. As parents, we never thought he would ever be released from prison to become our first democratically elected president. "Africa" is the name he carries as his mother's paternal last name, named after the continent Africa. When my son turned nine years old, he attended Acacia Park primary school, where most of the MP's children attended. The children called him "President." He returned home after school several afternoons and asked me if he would be a President one day.

"On the Run" is a poem about my four sisters and one brother. We were all actively involved in the struggle for liberation and were all affected because of our involvement. The poem is revealing the different experiences we had as a family. Some of us did not end up being detained. My brother at the age of 17 was found guilty of arson. It was alleged that he petrol bombed the local MP's house; he was sentenced to three years in prison, but he served one year and six months. My parents, politically conscious but not actively involved in the struggle, had to run from prison to hospital to court to support us after being detained by security police or beaten up by police.

GRAYSON and FALAIYE: What inspired you to start writing poetry?

AFRICA: My inspiration to start writing poetry in 1992 derived from the political situation in South Africa. As a black woman and a single parent, I experienced racial discrimination, as well as gender, social, economic and political discrimination. Poetry was (and still is) one way of dealing with one's anger, frustration, and difficulties.

GRAYSON and FALAIYE: What years did you serve as a member of the United Democratic Front (UDF)? Please describe the goals of the UDF and your participation in the organization.

AFRICA: I served as a member of the UDF from 1983-1990. The UDF was a powerful grassroots political movement inside South Africa that had firm links to the ANC (African National Congress). The UDF had been created to coordinate protest against the new apartheid constitution in 1983. It also coordinated protest against the first elections to the segregated Tricameral Parliament in 1984. It was a powerful organization that united over six hundred organizations, trade unions, church groups, community groups, and student organizations. In 1989, the UDF formed an alliance with the Congress of South African Trade Union organization (COSATU) to form the Mass Democratic Movement (MDM). The MDM began a countrywide defiance campaign of civil disobedience to challenge apartheid institutions. These organizations had been surrogates for the ANC inside South Africa, and the members were later integrated into organizations after the un-banning of the ANC in 1990.

I served as a member of the UDF branch in Ravensmead (formerly known as Tiervlei) in the Northern Suburbs of Cape Town. My participation in the UDF branch was to attend meetings and organize any form of action,[4] including protest marches, door-to-door canvassing, campaigns, throwing of stones or petrol bombs, burning of tires, pamphleteering, administrative duties, addressing rallies, and engaging the enemy, as well as our own people in our communities who supported the apartheid regime.

GRAYSON and FALAIYE: What are your additional experiences as an activist for social change in South Africa?

AFRICA: As a researcher and an agent for change, I was involved mainly in women's health research projects. The projects ranged from the experiences of women in arranging and undergoing second trimester abortion; intimate partner abuse of women; the accessibility and feasibility of medical abortions; reproductive health and social development interventions in Working for Water integrated rural development projects; and the validation of child mortality in the Western Cape. Other research projects include the development of career pathways for youth in the health and welfare sectors in relation to HIV/AIDS; immigration of health professionals; the role of traditional leaders in South Africa; and the characteristics of the relationship between post-graduate students and their supervisors.

GRAYSON and FALAIYE: What are some of the challenges you have experienced in South Africa?

AFRICA: The challenges I've experienced range from being black, a woman, single parent, careerist, comrade, and communist. I am still experiencing so many challenges in South Africa on a daily basis. These challenges are political, social, economic, and cultural. The constitution of South Africa including the Bill of Rights addresses inequalities between different race groups, sexes, and cultures. The reality is, as a black woman one still experiences sexism and racism. Inequalities between men and women still exist.

GRAYSON and FALAIYE: What are the primary changes that you have observed in South Africa over the past 20 years?

AFRICA: The political change within South Africa is one of the major changes I observed, from an apartheid state to a democratic one. Apartheid was adopted by the National Party after it came to power in 1948 as a system of racial segregation and domination. A basic aspect of apartheid was the exclusion of the majority from participation in central government on the basis of color. Since the mid-1970s, the apartheid regime has faced challenges from three directions: from the advancing forces of resistance and liberation amongst the majority denied freedom in South Africa; from the shifts in the balance of power in Southern Africa; and from the growing strength of the international movement against apartheid. Faced with these pressures and with economic decline, the regime was obliged to recognize the failure of its strategy and since 1985 began to speak of negotiations. In 1990, when the African National Congress and other organizations were un-banned, some political restrictions were lifted and Nelson Mandela was released. This was one of the first steps taken by the government in creating a climate for negotiations. The extent of the social problems were once again highlighted, which were created by apartheid and which a democratic government would have to address in dismantling the system. In 1994, South Africa had its first democratic elections. All racial policies were replaced with non-racial policies to heal the divisions of the past and establish a society based on democratic values, social justice, and fundamental human rights.

GRAYSON and FALAIYE: What lessons do you think the rest of the continent (Africa) can learn from the progress made in South Africa post-apartheid?

AFRICA: The attainment of democracy in 1994 presented the South African government with two challenges. First, significant institutional transformation and at the same time introducing new policies in line with the democratic Constitution. Second, while the government is dealing with the legacy of apartheid, it is facing new challenges of integrating the country in a rapidly changing global environment. Lessons the rest of the continent can learn is that the democratic state is able to exercise authority across society, and it enjoys legitimacy in the eyes of the overwhelming majority. Its capacity to formulate and implement policy, mobilize resources, frame and enforce laws, and the integrity of institutions—all indicate progress in governance. Furthermore, the Reconstruction and Development Programme (RDP) identified the following key objectives as very important for progress, and the rest of the continent should also focus on these objectives: meeting basic needs; building the economy; democratizing the state and society; developing human resources; and nation building.

I dedicate this poem to Thabo's late father, Desmond Links (1964-2004)

Thabo Nelson Africa
Lavinia Africa

They call you Thabo
Named after Deputy President
 Thabo Mbeki
You bring Happiness, Joy, Laughter
    My Son

Courageously asking if you could be a President
Courageously you accept my answer, yes
Intelligently your interest is politics
Intelligently as a nine year old,
    My Son

They call you Nelson
Named after our world renowned President
    Nelson Mandela
Your first cry into this Apartheid world. Eighteenth July
    My son

Assertively you ask me if you could be a President
Assertively you accept my answer, yes
Innocently your interest is politics
Innocently as a nine year old
    My son

They call you Africa
Black and beautiful Africa
You are as militant as Africa
Your spirit rise above Africa
    My Son
THABO NELSON AFRICA!!!

I dedicate this poem to my only brother Oswald James Africa

On The Run
Lavinia Africa

The eldest had to run
After many years of frustration
Seven months pregnant, on the run
To Johannesburg before detention

The second eldest had to run
From police brutality
Still, they caught and baton charged, on the run
To Tygerberg hospital

The third had to run
Police dogs chasing students in Oudtshoorn
Smacked in the face, on the run
Far away from home, the Capetonian

The fourth had to run
After petrol bomb explosion
With anger, because his sisters had to run
His tolerance and patience eroded

The second youngest had to run
Furthering the aims of a banned organization
In and out of court, on the run
The unfair treatment causes frustration

The youngest had to run
From solitary confinement
Alone, on the run
With all earnestly and commitment

The mother comradely had to run
With anger to Johannesburg
With anxiety to Tygerberg
With fear to Oudtshoorn

The father comradely had to run
With frustration to Riebeeck West
With mixed feelings to Bellville court
With militants to Brackenfell police station

Notes

1. This interview with Lavinia Africa was conducted by Sandra M. Grayson and Muyiwa Falaiye in November 2004.
2. Unified demonstration and expression of frustration through singing freedom songs.
3. Both poems are included after the interview.
4. Individuals volunteered to call together people in the neighborhood or community to discuss the political issues relevant for that community and in the broader context of the liberation struggle across the country and internationally.

3

Baton Charged

Lavinia Africa

One face, two faces, three faces
faces
more faces, white faces, camouflaged faces.

Who are they?
Where are they coming from?
What do they want here?
Why 30 white faces around me?

HELP! HELP!
I've been sent to the shop.
HELP! HELP!
I've done nothing wrong.

Black sticks for one Black body.
White bodies running to beat anybody.
They hit me as if I am nobody.

Unconscious falls the female black somebody.

Blood, Urine, Tears, Sweat!
Running down the Black body.
Fear, Anxiety, Anger, Hate!
Took over the Black beautiful face.

Unconscious
Thirty seconds I am awake
Run! Run!
Hurry! Hurry!
North, West, South or East.
Run or crawl is what I can do least.
Camouflaged faces passing slowly.
I should hurry or I will die.

One face, two faces, three faces
faces
more faces, black faces recognized faces.

Who are they?
Where are they staying?
Do they want to help me?
Why 30 Black faces around me?

Black pair of hands for one Black body.
Black bodies to help my body.
One of them catching me to save the body.
Unconscious falls the female Black somebody.

Thirty seconds—I'm awake
RUSH! RUSH!
MOVE! HURRY!
Warm water, clean cloth.
Stop blood, stop violence.
Emotions high, anger high.
Tygerberg Hospital on the Agenda High.

30 Black faces showed they care.
30 White camouflaged faces showed no care.

* * * * *

On the eve of the Tricameral Parliament elections in South Africa (21 August 1984), Lavinia Africa was a student activist and member of the United Democratic Front (UDF). In a small town, Ravensmead, in the Northern Suburbs of Cape Town, South Africa, a protest march was arranged for that date. She and her son's father, the late Desmond Links, were among the 200 protesters who were chased by police. She could not get away in time and, like many others, was severely *baton charged*, beaten with a police issued baton. The police used the baton during this political protest to beat the protesters until they were unconscious or dead, until they as police saw fit to stop.

4

Walking into the Sea
(For Walter Sisulu)

Chimalum Nwankwo

1

I know the burning bush offers us little
Because of the rising rage of omnivores

But Walter Sisulu saw much more
I will go singing was the song of his heart

With the terror of fangs now everywhere
From the warmest hearth to the sacred grove

Tumult has eaten the heart of silences
There are everywhere tent-poles of blood

But Walter Sisulu saw much more
I will go singing was the song of his heart

Do not take your bucket under the eaves
The sound on the roof is a rain of blood

Do not wander toward the old village spring
The sliver sand glows with the radiance of death

But Walter Sisulu saw much more
I will go singing was the song of his heart

Do not seek the shade of the great iroko
The old iron roots sit on cotton and sand

My dreams are tortures of vanishing fruits
No name fruits from the vanishing trees

But Walter Sisulu saw much more
I will go singing was the song of his heart

Passing like the gods from this prison of fire
Like the last sweet music of a great festival

When flutes in the breeze wail ever so softly

After the thunder of drums and stamping of feet
After the ecstasy from the blaze of transition

The braids of wails with the laces of delight
Strangely touched by some strained memories

Walter Sisulu has gone on marching
I will go singing was the song of his heart

Walter Sisulu embraced Apartheid prisons
Like the noble black slaves did old Ibo Landing

Life is life when life is without fear
The prison of fire breaks at the sound of that song

Walter Sisulu! Walter Sisulu!
Why did those demons tremble at your name

2

My sister's heart is the domain of vultures
My brother's limb is the sinew of jackals

My mother forgets the nights of moon glow
My father begs in the open for offals

But for Walter Sisulu who saw much more
I will go singing was the song of his heart

The mornings shake with riots of relatives
Evenings heave with the threat of sorrows

Nights are no more for our pillows of rest
The curtains rise then for demon nightmares

I hear the voices of those waltzing with my foes
Their plea is of life in the belly of the whale

But for Walter Sisulu who saw much more
I will go singing was the song of his heart

It is a marriage of the most wicked spirits
When nights of terror marry days of evil

The miracle dwells there in the triumphant roars
In the approvals of the complacent silences

In the coronations of the bloody chieftains
In the rains of stars when an angel crashes

The burning bush offers no shelter no shade
Because of the rising rage of omnivores

Walter Sisulu did not blink at the demons
With chains on ankles and chains on wrists

Like the noble slaves at old Ibo Landing
Who saw all the demons and did not blink

Walter Sisulu stared through fire and smoke
I will go singing was the song of his heart

3

Walter Sisulu! Walter Sisulu!
When the storms rise over the highest iroko

And the sky is howling pieces of glass
I will walk calmly into the deepest blue sea

And let the sea turn into molten magma
A boiling Jupiter come hurtling down my head

I know the kind of heart and head I will need
Faces and names which turn danger to stone

Walter Sisulu! Walter Sisulu!
All those who go singing like you

I will invoke all the slaves at Ibo Landing
I will call your name like the early morning cock

I will face the teeth of all the omnivores
I will not blink at the terror of their eyes

At the fire and smoke of the burning bush
And at the rising rage of all the omnivores

I will go singing like Walter Sisulu
Walter Sisulu! Walter Sisulu!

The voice of your soul will be my guide
My music the chains from the limbs of slaves

Into freedom's arms and the wings of light
I will smash the gates of the prisons of fire

Like an arrow straight into the heart of the sun
I will go singing like Walter Sisulu . . .

5

Politics of Multilingualism in South Africa

Alosi J. M. Moloi

Africans in South Africa/Azania are rapidly losing their languages because of a misguided idea that economic development and civilization in general depend on the English language. Calculated efforts by subtle agents of white privilege and continued domination are encouraging this false notion. African languages and traditions are essential, must be central, and should be taught in colleges and universities. There are dangers inherent in carelessly and blindly entrusting the education of African children to the hands of those holding black people in contempt while marginalizing African languages and cultures. Sadly, even though South Africa/Azania has proclaimed eleven official languages, many African children have moved away from the African core, having forgotten their mother tongue and traditions. African parents can play a significant role to reverse this dangerous process by teaching their children the significance and beauty of African heritage and traditional languages. Africans will prevail only as a united group with a common purpose, values, traditions, and strong leaders, sending African children to schools that honor, celebrate, and respect African languages, culture, and dignity. African homes must be strongholds of African languages. The current trend of marginalizing African languages must be combated.

Background Facts about Multilingualism in South Africa

Africans have always tolerated language differences. In fact, we pride ourselves on our linguistic richness and our willingness to learn other people's languages. We negotiate a multilingual environment everyday of our lives without feeling inferior to those whose languages we have learned. Basotho learned Tsonga, Venda, and the Nguni languages, and vice-versa, without cowing down to "outsiders." Indeed, having competence in several different languages brought honor and prestige to the multi-linguists and enriched cultural relations. That was the situation among various African linguistic groups before an outsider settler group, the Europeans, began to propagate their spurious claim of white supremacy and exploit cultural differences to arbitrarily create unfair advantages for themselves at the expense of Africans. European abuses, brutality, callousness, repression, excesses, and political torture, assured them the dominant political, economic, and social position. Next, their languages, English and Afrikaans, were presented as the superior languages, not because of any innate or inherent superiority quality in them, but because they were languages of the group that violently and arbitrarily appropriated social, political, and economic prestige. Therefore, their social, political, and economic prestige and power were conferred on their languages and all Europeans who had done nothing, but had only the color of skin that associated them with the despotic rulers. Thus, through unearned privilege, even the poorest, uncouth, uneducated, unemployed, and/or ignorant Briton or Boer, or their cousins, claimed racial superiority and linguistic dominance. Language, the European form, had become a weapon to subjugate and exploit Africans. It was deemed good for the Africans to know English and Afrikaans, but not to claim equality with the whites.

Missionary schools, and later Bantu education "concentration" camps masquerading as schools, focused on producing a subjugated community that would not challenge for their rightful place, side by side with other ethnic groups in South Africa. The missionaries, in particular, observed the infamous segregation policies more than their Christian doctrines. Their belief, just like that of the larger settler community, was that the African was not destined to rule, or to have a say in the government of the country. Thus, to them, it was pointless and dangerous that Africans should become so educated that they would be in a position to see and to regard no white supremacy myth. Therefore, the curriculum was designed in such a manner to produce a small elitist group that was alienated from their roots, the African masses. They became black Englishmen, a hybrid class, with one foot on white culture and the other, precariously tipping on African tradition.

With the advent of Bantu education in 1953, whites in South Africa revealed their true colors, their hatred and contempt for the Africans.[1] The racialists were bent on humiliating Africans. After all, the all white so-called Inter-departmental Committee on Native Education (1935-1936) had long declared that regarding education the white child was being prepared for life in a dominant society, while the black child for life in a subordinate society. The curriculum was redesigned for the Africans, emphasizing vocational training, domestic science (home economics), arts and crafts, religious instruction, and gardening. Examinations and rote learning became the characteristics of learning process in African schools, discouraging critical analysis or thinking. Diligence, obedience, and humility were qualities emphasized, with the whole content of education designed to reshape African minds to serve whites unquestioningly. Ill-trained, ill-informed, underpaid, and demoralized teachers were unleashed on the Africans to enforce parrot-like memorizations. Therefore, the opponents of missionary schools and the racialist enemies of the African had seized the opportunity to enforce a system of State controlled Bantu education, which would numb the African brain. The envisaged product of the new experiment, Bantu education, was a semi-educated African, with no aspirations whatsoever, except to serve the whites.

The architect of Bantu Education, Dr. W. W. M. Eiselen, hoped to chain the African only to traditional tribal culture while isolating him or her from the international scene. To give Bantu Education a cloak of legitimacy and to hide its evil and immoral motive, Eiselen distorted sound education principles. While it is an axiom that the child learns best in his or her own mother tongue, that language should have developed acceptable terminology to be used in any sound school which is aimed at creating a whole person, not a local, provincial, and narrow-minded man or woman. In their haste to enforce Bantu Education, Eiselen and his cohorts demanded use of African languages only, not the revered languages, but concoctions that had hurriedly been cooked up by hastily set up "Language Boards" for new terminologies. For example, a language that is neither Sesotho, nor Sepedi, nor Setswana, would be used as a medium of instruction for Basotho, Bapedi, or Batswana children. This so-called official "Bantu language" was formed by whites who claimed to know African languages more than the Africans themselves; hence they dominated the language boards. Teachers who did not know this concocted language were forced to use the newly-coined terms while also being terrorized by brainwashed, apolitical, subservient African local school committees. African education was thus stunted, confused, and stifled. Reflecting the sinister intentions of the whites in South Africa, Dr. Hendrik Vervoerd (the architect of racial segregation in South Africa) insisted that Africans must be broken to serve white interests and should be made willing collaborators in their own enslavement. The Boer government sought total control of African schools to closely supervise, dictate, and enforce the enslaving curriculum, instruction, and "assessment." Whites wanted to destroy African identity, confidence, and languages. Without their languages, and, therefore, without a clear frame of reference and identity, our people might unintentionally become willing collaborators in their own dehumanization and oppression. In a 1954 speech, the Honorable Mangaliso Robert Sobukwe, founding President of the Pan-Africanist Congress of Azania (PAC), had rightly observed that whites in South Africa could maintain continued domination only by enlisting the active cooperation of the oppressed.[2] Sobukwe organized and mobilized the masses to resist. Numerous Africans fought in the resistance movement.

The Politics of Language and the "New" Elite in South Africa

A "nation" that does not know its history can unintentionally become a willing collaborator in its own enslavement. It remains weak, divided and impotent—historically and politically insignificant. In South Africa during times of national pride, unity, historical purpose and mission in the kingdoms of the Basotho, AmaZulu, AmaXhosa, Bapedi, Bavenda, AmaSwati and Batswana, our cultures and languages provide answers about life, and the enemies were kept in check. However, during national uncertainty, the enemies became bold. They advanced, mobilized, attacked and scattered people, then proceeded to entrench themselves, imposing their languages and conventions. The Anti-ArnaXhosa, Anti-AmaZulu, Anti-Bapedi and Anti-Basotho wars are cases in point.

Reading old Southern African publications such as *Isiaidimi samaXhosa* (The AmaXhosa Messenger) in the 1870s or *Izwi laBantu* (The Voice of the People)[3] and *Leselinyana* (Light/Wisdom)[4] reveals many uncertainties, lack of confidence, confusion, mimicry and blunders among the new elite and products of the missionary schools. Some of them viewed tradition negatively, while European imperialism and pillaging by whites were seen as positive missions. Some, such as a man named Elijah Makiwane[5] at some point, actually believed that Shakespeare, Francis Bacon, John Milton, and other Western cultural products, were the means to civilization. They even went as far as to accuse traditional rulers as impediments to "Progress," calling the gallant resistance to anti-AmaXhosa wars "irrational." They became poor carbon copies of the Europeans, mimicking their mannerisms, and even acquiring European names for presumed prestige. The sad story continued in the early 1900s, the 1920s, and the 1930s as African intellectuals attempted to find their place in a Euro-centric, brutal and oppressive environment. In a letter (22 August 2004) to the editor of *Sunday World*, a Johannesburg newspaper, Thabile Mange of Kagiso Township, Krugersdorp refers to the destructive practice of the new elite who address the people in technical jargon and exaggerated words and expect the masses to understand. She also laments that we are doing nothing while the Afrikaners, our former oppressors, are fighting a fierce battle to protect their language and culture.

Nevertheless, there were other gallant Africans such as the great leaders of the Ethiopian Movement, including Nehemiah Tile, Mangena Mokone, and Pambani Jeremiah Mzimba in the 19th century who began to focus on self-definition, development, and defense. They studied carefully the remarkable achievements of African Americans who had been brutalized by slavery, a crime against humanity, and the despicable "Jim Crow Law." They vehemently rejected white supremacy claims, seeing them for the nonsense they are, and refused to succumb to the false claim of alleged African inferiority. In fact, these men proclaimed, loud and clear, that it would be suicidal if African languages and traditions are forsaken for the English language. Everyone should learn from the past and change course. African languages and heritage are essential and must be central; they are the languages of African history, ancestors, land, heritage and soul.

The legacy of apartheid and racism remains a serious threat, especially to youth who have been co-opted to perpetuate a culture of failure and poverty. Getting crumbs from the white man's table and materialism have become motivating factors in the lives of many youth, making some of them put their greed before the interests and aspiration of their people. Those who are perpetuating white privilege and domination know this, and they are encouraging it! White privilege and economic injustice for the Africans persist in South Africa. Parents, educators, and politicians must work hard to reverse this dangerous, intolerable situation; wake up from this deep sleep brought about by euphoria of multi-ethnic, non-racial elections since 1994; and realize that struggle is constant and continuous, and far from being over. The enemies of African dignity and humanity, and the active agents of Euro-centric domination, are timelessly working to create "Negroes" in Africa, with no self-identity, national frame of reference, group pride, language, or desire for upliftment, but always diligently working to do the perceived master's biding.

Conclusion

It is obvious that the prestige and power possessed by a group can be arbitrarily projected through their language. Myths are often created to convince the perceived subordinate group that its economic survival and well-being are dependent on abandoning its own language and cultural heritage. However, no language is inherently superior or inferior despite haughty pretenses of the supremacists. Africans should continue their fight to preserve their cultural heritage and languages. Whites, through their corporations and grip on the purse strings, are striving for white privilege and perpetual subjugation of the African masses. African languages are arrogantly seen as threatening white standards as a strong African, confident in his/her culture and language, cannot become a native puppet that needs to be regulated by the white master. Despite the fact that all along the Africans have coped well with challenges of multilingualism in the universities, the new overseers, in the guise of academicians and corporate captains, want us to mimic the "herrenvolk" dialect to be acceptable to them. Despite claims to the contrary, a single variety of English does not exist—not even in England, aside from the pretense of the "upper crust" to enforce their dialect! So, why should Africans abandon their languages? Why all the nonsense of the haughty, presumptuous academicians and business captains? Why English competency should be demanded as a requirement for admission to schools such as Rhodes University when South Africa recognizes eleven official languages? India has nineteen, Switzerland three, the European Union eleven national languages, without a fuss. So, what's the motivation of the new colonizers? Why do they hold African languages in contempt? In "Hostage to Hope," an article published on 23 August 2004 in the *Sowetan* (a Johannesburg daily newspaper), Eddy Maloka is critical of this spurious superiority pretense of the whites in South Africa who are still dreaming of English imperialism and asks how long this nonsense will persist.[6]

In the New South Africa we must be vigilant for subtle tricks intended to perpetuate white supremacy myths. Those with prestige and power are exploiting cultural and linguistics difference to artificially create unfair advantages for themselves and their kind. In short, as others have observed, white privilege is intertwined with economic injustice for the Africans. Africans must fight fiercely to protect our languages and culture and carefully study African history. African children must move toward the African core and learn African languages. African languages, heritage, and dignity must be honored, celebrated, and respected. We must urgently return to our African roots and heritage. A people without their own languages will always be a carbon copy and door mat for sinister oppressors. Therefore, we must rescue African languages, history, value systems, and cultures.

Notes

1. For further details see Moloi's "Bantu Education and Politics in South Africa" in *Journal of the Black Experience and Pan-African Issues* 1.4 (Winter 1975).
2. Speech by the Honorable Mangaliso Robert Sobukwe, President of the Pan Africanist Congress of Azania (South Africa) in Johannesburg, May 1959.
3. These were publications that served the new products of missionary schools in the 19th century and early 20th century.
4. A publication in the Kingdom of Lesotho since the 1870s.
5. Elijah Makiwane was an influential editor of *Isigidimi samaXhosa* in the 1870s. He became President of the Native Educational Association in 1884. That premier organization for the African intellectuals was founded in 1879. Since "education" was available only in English, some of the new elites erroneously believed in the alleged superiority of English as a civilizing agent. His views are explained in Elijah Makiwane, "Five Months in Pondomisi-land," *Imvo ZaBatsudu* (African Opinion) 26 January, 3 February, 10 February, 1886.
6. Reverend Mangena Maake Mokone was a leading member of the Ethiopian Movement in South Africa. Mokone, along with Pambani Jeremiah Mzimba, played a key role in establishing links with the AME Church in the U.S. and forged lasting links with African Americans in general in the 19th century. These men were also members of the Native Educational Association.

Works Cited

Makiwane, Elijah. "Five Months in Pondomisiland." *Imvo ZaBatsudu* (African Opinion) 26 January, 3 February, and 10 February 1886.

Maloka, Eddy. "Hostage to Hope." *Sowetan* 23 August 2004.

Mange, Thabile. "Letter to the Editor." *Sunday World* 22 August 2004.

"Report of the Interdepartmental Committee on Native Education, 1935-1936." Pretoria: Government Printer, 1936.

6

Reunion at the Jazz Castle

7 August 2000

Patric Tariq Mellet

My brother Mervyn Afrika[1]
that was one hellava set
that Knysna Blue medley
with old Robbie's hey ya hey ya hoh!
Vernon's Jazz Castle aflamed
Lorca's duende stirring it up
returning to the Jolly Carp[2] roots
the old roots of Cape Town
over 20 years of exile receding.
In the old days we used to say WE DON'T KNOW (OSWIETIE)
now we can say WE KNOW (OSWIET)
but Mervyn then you told me
No man my brother Pat
we can now say WE KNOW MORE! (OSWIET MEER)

Notes

1. Mervyn Africa, one of South Africa's finest Jazz pianists (he plays what he calls the African piano), returned to South Africa in August 2000 after over twenty years in exile in the United Kingdom. Mervyn played in two bands in the old days—Spirits Rejoice and Oswietie. This *cameo of captured time* was inspired by a reunion performance at Vernon's Jazz Castle; the event was a homecoming celebration for Mervyn Africa.
2. Jolly Carp was an old jazz venue of the late 1960s and early 1970s.

7

Voice in the New South Africa

Ronald Dorris

In summer 2000, I was selected to participate in the United States/South Africa National Cultural Heritage and Technology Training program. The three-year funding for this initiative was provided by the Ford and Mellon foundations, and the program was overseen by Michigan State University. Given a total of thirty interns, twenty-four were from South Africa and the six of us from the United States worked at historically black colleges and universities. The interns from South Africa visited the U.S. in July 2000. The U.S. interns were charged with working on a project that could be implemented in South Africa. In summer 2002, I was in South Africa for six weeks. The first four weeks were spent in Durban where I delivered a lecture on cultural and intellectual studies at Kwa Muhle Museum and a similar lecture at Natal Museum in Pietermaritzburg. At the University of Durban-Westville, I conducted a one-week short-short story workshop with ten students from KwaZulu Natal province and one from Zimbabwe. With a supplemental grant from Intercultural and International Programs at Xavier University of Louisiana, I spent the final two weeks in Johannesburg. I delivered a keynote address at the Johannesburg Art Gallery during the opening of the exhibition *"Amabal' Engwe*: Traditional Garments of the Southern

African Region." I also visited Pretoria, Eersterus, Alexandra, and Soweto.

My interest in flying across the Atlantic Ocean involved a search for VOICE in the new South Africa. For eight years, the country had been rid of overt colonial control. How does the average man, woman, and child sound a note that is the new South Africa? Traveling the national highways at turbo engine speed, gazing at the myriad skyscrapers, observing thousands of people on cell phones or listening to music performed by artists from the United States, I had the impression that in Durban I was in Los Angeles and in Johannesburg I was in New York. It is the voice of the people that I sought. To hear the voice of the people, I chose "to remain one with the people." The best way to do this is to take a daily ride in a *four/four* that transports fourteen to sixteen individuals. One simply does not get any closer than this to hear voice. Who speaks for the people? Do they speak for self? How does one hear them? I engaged brothers and sisters in myriad conversation about VOICE in the new South Africa. Our conversations began to flow toward a common concern that the universal that the spirit seeks is charged with maintaining its freedom. As we reflected on art behind glass cases in museums and in boutique shops owned by "foreigners" while the indigenous artist is bypassed on the street, we raised the cry about whether a new knowledge can be put into an entity by association.

Query about VOICE in the new South Africa led us to consider what a performance is to people inside a culture and what it is to those outside the culture. We focused on performance relative to ritual, how the traditional serves to forge a continual link that breeds familiarity and education. In particular, I proposed that inside culture ritual constitutes embracing time and place, and outside culture ritual constitutes occupying space. I accept that *time* and *place* are ways of life, energy that can be transported anywhere and transformed for production to take place. On the other hand, I surmise that *space* simply is allocated boundary. To advance my position, I shared in discourse with sisters and brothers a point of view posited by Jean Toomer, an African American and artist whose works initially were published during the 1920s; his papers are currently housed at the Beinecke Rare Books and Manuscript Library, Yale University. In one of his sketches housed at Yale University, Toomer surmises that humans are instrumental in generating constant interaction among themselves, the land, and the soul of a region so that growth can take place. His account informs that within the circle that encompasses life and death, one disavows the occupying of space (possibilities) by embracing cross fertilization with time and place (actualization).[1] To sound my note for promotion of voice in the new South Africa, I centered discourse on South African history and culture in congruence with the study of cultural constructs. I used the following explanation as a working definition of *cultural construct*: when a pattern of thinking and doing that permeates the activities of a people is combined with the distinctive human mode of building a structure so that a network of daily routine is centered around that structure, a cultural construct evolves. A cultural construct so occupies the activities of a people that it lends itself a quality of lasting duration, either manifested in the actual structure or manifested in art, legend, and folklore among other social engagements and historical accounts.

As a reference point for discourse relative to VOICE, I focused on the levee that holds back the water of the mighty Mississippi River. Its design and use complement a way of life rather than its being a useless and imposed structure that has no value in the life or permeability of a people. I then presented parallel assessment about how *Amabal' Engwe*: Traditional Garments of the Southern African Region could be studied as a cultural construct in congruence with cultural and intellectual studies— the impact of ideas that influenced production of the clothes; material culture study—the tools used to manufacture the clothes; regionalism and popular culture study. Once the exhibition was cast in a broader context for discussion, those of us assembled were able to "lift" the garments out of glass cases and, via time and place, transport these objects beyond space. In such context, VOICE emerged. As our discussions relative to voice continued, I encouraged everyone to embrace the idea that in our own life story we are an *autos* (a self) and a *bios* (a life)—hence the word *autobiography*. As a self we are an actor for permanence and change. Life as process is the agent whereby transformation takes place. Turning to Toomer's writings in *The Wayward and the Seeking*, I drew from Toomer's philosophy as an angle to focus on how one might connect with VOICE. Toomer posited that when one is forced into extremes, tensions arise. He believed that tensions multiply when the order brought to bear on environment and person is directed from fabricated measures instead of Natural Law. Toomer believed that it would be to the advantage of the individual to put tensions into perspective instead of becoming overwhelmed by fragmentation. Thus he distinguished between tensions generated from Natural Law as opposed to those that arise from artificial opposition.[2]

Toomer also believed that when one connects with self to embrace an inherent aristocracy of character (not as a social aristocrat but as an aristocrat of culture, spirit, and ideas) an inaugural stage of a great cultural phase begins—sounding a note whereby each individual has a part to play. Rather than adjust to our life with only the personal in view, Toomer believed that we should become aware of the broader humanity calling us.[3] In terms of the broader humanity calling the African in the United States, Toomer expressed concern for a people who, by sharing a common experience, give rise to a common ideal. To embrace this ideal, Toomer argued that Africans in the United States must be made aware of the subtle intuitive natures of their own qualities. Toomer believed it was his duty and privilege to aid, perhaps in large measure, to crystallize an African American ideal. He explained that motives for actual creation of this ideal were not social because anything vital in the way of writing must be the cause of effects that lie outside the province of art. He viewed art as social—how people appropriate or misappropriate what has been created. The inherent process of creating the art he saw as spiritual. In being true to one's nature, Toomer observed, one then is true to the nature of others because they are part of the social whole.[4]

To study the inherent process of how art was and is created can give rise to VOICE in any culture. I am privileged to have been a participant in discourse in the new South Africa. My colleagues and I have pledged "to remain one with the people" so that our respective life and work collectively draw from art and humanity to help both the spectator and the performer gauge the difference between *reaction* and *response*. When I returned to the United States, I received an article from one brother whose work, now published, focuses on the economic aspect of historical African art. Examination is centered on the process of production, acquisition of materials, means of exchange to acquire materials, design inherent in work, and education passed on from generation to generation that enables production and design to be ongoing. My sisters and brothers in South Africa pay homage to the great Zulu warrior Shaka, crediting the spirit of his wisdom for bringing us together as collaborators who now are casting assessment of historical works in a broader context. Among others, we take our cue from a position advanced by George Brandon in *Santeria from Africa to the New World: The Dead Sell Memories*:

> Through cultural performances a culture achieves a separate vision of itself and may create a canvas on which it paints a picture of what life would be like if people could change how they lived with each other or even the very nature of their own individual lives. (Brandon 143)

Casting assessment of historical African works in the broader context of cultural construct can help to paint such pictures and to sound a continuous note of liberation. May the ancestors continue to guide and to inspire Africans throughout the Diaspora as we embrace VOICE that emerges in the new South Africa.

Notes

1. Jean Toomer Papers (JTP), Sketch, 49:2, n.d.
2. Toomer, Jean. "Reflections of an Earth-Being." *The Wayward and the Seeking: A Collection of Writings by Jean Toomer.* Ed. Darwin Turner. 20.
3. JTP 20:514, Outline of an Autobiography, n.d., 37-44.
4. JTP 9:283, Jean Toomer to Mae Wright, 4 August 1922.

Works Cited

Brandon, George. *Santeria from Africa to the New World: The Dead Sell Memories.* Bloomington: Indiana University Press, 1997.

Toomer, Jean. Letter to Mae Wright. 4 August 1922. Jean Toomer Papers. Beinecke Rare Books and Manuscript Library, Yale University, New Haven.

———. Outline of an Autobiography. N.d. Jean Toomer Papers. Beinecke Rare Books and Manuscript Library, Yale University, New Haven.

———. "Reflections of an Earth-Being." *The Wayward and the Seeking: A Collection of Writings by Jean Toomer.* Ed. Darwin Turner. Washington, DC: Howard University Press, 1983.

———. Sketch. N.d. Jean Toomer Papers. Beinecke Rare Books and Manuscript Library, Yale University, New Haven.

Turner, Darwin, ed. *The Wayward and the Seeking: A Collection of Writings by Jean Toomer.* Washington, DC: Howard University Press, 1983.

8

Engineering Patriotism:
Americanization and Afrikanerization

Patrick Rankhumise

Among the parallels that can be drawn between *Americanization* in North America and *Afrikanerization* in South Africa are the ways that these policies promoted like-mindedness relative to social, political, cultural, and economic development in both countries.[1] In the following commentary, I will define and contextualize the concepts of focus and briefly discuss background on the nature of human interaction relative to these two concepts. The goal is to analyze similarities between Afrikaner and American nationalism debates and development post-World War I.

Americanization involves encouraging citizens to become loyal to the United States. Emphasis centers on the importance of encouraging citizens to place national interest above ethnic background in the United States of America, a nation replete with immigrants. As the Americanization process unfolded, former U.S. president Woodrow Wilson posited that Americans must have a consciousness different from the other nations in the world. During the same historical period in the Union of South Africa, the Afrikaners wanted to develop solidarity in order to deter social, political, and cultural domination by the English and the nonwhites. The concern of being dominated by these groups led to the rise of

the Afrikanerisation project. In the context of this analysis, Afrikanerization is defined as a movement intended to promote a common identity for
a body of white citizens, who chronicle their presence in South Africa
since the occupation of the pre-anglicized Cape Peninsula. The Dutch
settlers, who later named themselves Afrikaners, controlled this area.
Both the white Americans and Afrikaners, perceived blacks as inferior
and discriminated against and oppressed black people.

From 1880 to the eve of World War I, the U.S. federal government
(fearing to be outnumbered by the blacks) encouraged immigration from
Europe. Many among the new Europeans arrivals, however, retained
their psychological bond to their respective native countries. Thus the
United States accelerated growth in the white population with "hyphen-
ated-Americans" (including German-Americans, Italian-Americans,
French-Americans). When the United States entered World War I on the
side of the allied powers, it became difficult for the country to convince a
number of hyphenated Americans who sympathized with their original
homelands to take arms against their own people. The existence of some
citizens' dubious dedication to the United States became a threat to
North America's then newly acquired status as a super power in the post-
war period. The American government established a commission on
Americanization. This ultimately led to encouraging all whites living in
the country to swear their allegiance to the U.S. The United States has
always viewed itself as "the" America; through the promotion of the
program of Americanization, citizens were encouraged to commit themselves to live and die for the United States, even if this meant waging
wars against their nation of origin. As the Americanization process unfolded, the African Americans remained at the lowest layer of the American social, economic, cultural, and political pyramids.

Americanization promoted that citizens use English as their primary
language, embrace American culture, consume American products, and
place the United States above all other nations of the world. As oppression continued to be directed against African Americans, there also continued to be a strong African American protest movement against white
domination. For example, in the 1920s the world was exposed to the philosophy of Marcus Garvey, who relocated to the United States from Ja-
maica and incorporated in New York his Universal Negro Improvement
Association (UNIA). Such protest efforts later served as models and inspiration for African American leaders such as Malcolm X and Martin
Luther King, Jr. While protest has contributed significantly to enable
African Americans to secure civil liberties, persistent oppression against
African Americans continues, especially with regard to economics and

politics.

In South Africa, the Afrikaners controlled political power since 1910, when two Boer republics of Transvaal and Orange Free State were merged with the two British colonies in Cape and Natal. By that time, the Africans had suffered two losses at the hands of the British both following two South African Wars (1886 and 1889). The Afrikaner defeat in those wars, and their loss of the Cape and Natal, was received with mixed feelings. Some sectors of the Afrikaner population perceived that cooperation with the English, and other people of European descent, was vital to maintaining white supremacy over the Africans and other non-white groups. The experiences at the hands of the British, and the Afrikaner's quest to subordinate the black communities and ultimately gain socio-economic and cultural domination in South Africa, can account for the rise of Afrikanerdom (Afrikanerness).

The period from 1920 to 1930 was turbulent in so far as the development of Afrikaner nationalism was concerned. The South African Party, which retained friendly relations with the English, cherished the creation of a unified white nation, which was to maintain white supremacy in the Union of South Africa. White unity in the context of this group entailed both communities "forgiving and forgetting" past differences and collaborating to create white South African nationalism. This ideology was opposed by the National Party, which perceived the Afrikaners as an organic ethnic group set on defending their ethnic interests. Under the leadership of Dr. Daniel Francois Malan, the Afrikaners renamed their party the Purified National Party, thus justifying their total unwillingness to merge with any non-Afrikaner group.

The "purified" Afrikaners believed that it was impossible for them to "forgive and forget" the aftermath of the two South African Wars and how the British took the Cape and Natal from them. This Afrikaner population organized themselves with the intent of maintaining their ethnic purity and endeavored to fight for and sustain the Afrikaner social, political, cultural, and economic domination of other groups in the Union of South Africa. This principle was reflected in the Purified National Party 1938 election caption which appealed to pure Afrikaners to vote the party in order the rid the Afrikaner nation of "foreign" elements. It further warned Afrikaner women to avoid sexual relationships and marriage to Africans.

Various measures were put in place to encourage the Afrikanerization process. For example, the Afrikanerization process can be paralleled with the rise of German nationalism during the era of Adolph Hitler. Like Hitler's version of German nationalism, Afrikanization was based on racial superiority, similar to the German concept of "Aryan race." The Afrikaners, on the other hand, called themselves the *herrenvolk* (God's nations), which was destined to bring civilization to those they perceived as barbaric and uncivilized. *Taalbeweging*, an Afrikaans language movement, was launched with the intention of making the Afrikaner population appear literate in their own language. Secondly, Afrikaner cultural organizations were established to entrench Afrikanerdom among the population. Such organizations included the Broederbond and the Ossewa-Brandwag. These were some of the measures promoted to encourage Afrikaners to embrace a consciousness different from the consciousness of every other ethic group in the Union of South Africa and in the world. Currently, such consciousness persists within some Afrikaner movements, including the Afrikaner Weerstandige Beweging (AWB) and the Boeremag.

The Afrikaners in South Africa lost political power following the birth of a democratic South Africa in 1994. Within the Afrikaner polity, this loss of power was received with mixed feelings. One brand accepted the transition and endeavored to use democratic processes to maintain their rights. Others decided not to accept the democratic transition and started to conduct terror activities intended to overthrow the democratically elected government. This faction represents a branch within the Afrikaner polity, which wants to wage anarchy in South Africa in order to restore "the" Afrikaner domination.[2]

Notes

1. During Fall 2002, the Department of African American Studies at Xavier University of Louisiana invited me to present my paper titled "Democratization in Africa: The Case of Kenya." The invitation was issued to coincide with Black History Month in February 2003. As part of my visit that February, I presented lectures to undergraduate students on the plight of Africans in (South) Africa. Among others, I had the privilege of attending an interdisciplinary studies class on cultural and intellectual history of the 1920s titled "The Harlem Renaissance Movement;" the course was taught by the award-winning scholar Dr. Ronald Dorris. On the day I attended, the lecture focused on the "Americanization project," which refers to strategies employed by the U.S. federal government after World War I to convert citizens and those not naturalized to embrace the policy of 100% Americanism. The

governing principle of this policy of Americanism was "making citizens alike forever."

2. As a starting place for additional information on *Americanization* in North America and *Afrikanerization* in South Africa, see the following texts:

Alba, Richard D. and Victor Nee. *Remaking the American Mainstream: Assimilation and Contemporary Immigration*. Cambridge: Harvard University Press, 2003.

Kraut, Alan M. *The Huddled Masses: The Immigrant in American Society, 1880-1921*. Arlington Height: Harlan Davidson, Inc., 1982.

Marks, Shula and Stanley Trapido, eds. *The Politics of Race, Class and Nationalism in the Twentieth Century South Africa*. London: Longman, 1987.

O'Meara, Dan. *Volkskapitalisme: Class, Capital and Ideology in the Development of Afrikaner Nationalism 1934-1948*. Johannesburg: Ravan Press, 1983.

Pedraza, Silvia and Ruben Rumbaut, eds. *Origins and Destinies: Immigration, Race, and Ethnicity in America*. Belmont: Wadsworth Press, 1996.

9

Economic Aspects of African Art

Prince Mbusi Dube

Having thrown off the shackles of apartheid, everywhere change is taking place in South Africa. By an overwhelming majority, the African National Congress won the multi-racial elections in 1994. The cry on the lips of many who traverse the byways and highways is who or what constitutes VOICE in the new South Africa. VOICE emerges in various forms and tones, not the least of which is how traditional African artworks are displayed in museum collections. One way to project VOICE in the new South Africa is the call to view museum collections in broader contexts. Previously, exhibits in museums were showcased in a way that demeaned people of African descent and potentially scared children who visited a gallery.

Currently, although limited by resources at their disposal, curators at a number of museums dispense justice to collections and to visitors. Considering the economic aspect of historical African art (or what is referred to as traditional African art), it is important to note that such collections at museums throughout the world are disputable. A significant number of these artworks were stolen from Africa when invaders from around the globe went on looting sprees, kidnapping intellectuals and artists and stealing property. These artworks are now housed in various museums, generating income for foreign nations, whereas the economies of African nations from whence these works were stolen endure economic hardship. Inclusive in such collections are works by African people who were barred by white colonial powers from accessing mineral resources, such as diamond and gold, in a way previously utilized. It became a crime to acquire or possess such materials, which were means to the production of African art.

A number of collections around the world house the product of a tormented people who could not travel at will, and scholars who could not do research. Continental communication had been broken down. Trading with other nations no longer was feasible. This must be kept in mind when viewing certain holdings. Today an African who wants to see genuine historical African art has to raise money to travel to a foreign country to see what his or her ancestors produced.

When I was growing up in the hinterlands of Northern KwaZulu/Natal, my grandmother always engaged in creative work during her spare time. Her favorite activity was to make *amacansi* (straw mats) for family use. It never dawned on me that she was an artist. Although experienced in that field, she always would buy *amacansi* from someone else, especially for a special occasion such as a wedding. This confused me. Why would she buy from someone else what she could make. I did not look at this exchange from an economic point of view.

Apart from devoting attention to the market value of historical African art works, there are important issues to consider relative to economic elements of the work. When viewing historical African art works in a museum display, one should consider the process of production. When analyzing an object made out of beads, one does not have to think only about color combination, functionality of the object, or who used the object in what era. One also can devote attention to original utensils used and material used to make those utensils. How historical African art was fashioned can help one to appreciate the function and value of these works. If utensils to produce these works were not found in a respective locality, one can trace place of origin. For example, we have been taught that beads came from outside Africa, but new evidence points to KMT (Egypt), emphasizing the argument that vibrant economic activity was taking place in Africa a millennia ago. The type of trade conducted when these art works were produced needs to be taken into consideration. Although capable of producing what was needed, some people preferred to buy from other producers.

It is known that Africans sailed to America before Columbus. King Abubakari of Mali was one of the first to organize expeditions to sail across the Atlantic Ocean. "He surrounded himself with people of like mind. Scholars of Timbuktu who entertained theories of a gourd-shaped world and dreamed of lands beyond waters" (Van Sertima 43). In 1310, experienced boat makers were called to the king's palace to discuss the possibility of making his dream a reality. A site was chosen along the seacoast of Senegambia for the boat building operation. Two hundred master boats and two hundred supply boats were built. Supply boats stored food, such as dried meat and grain and preserved fruits in huge ceramic jars. Gold and other items of trade were also stored. Don Juan, the King of Portugal, initially informed Columbus about the secret trade route that the Africans had been traveling. Native Americans offered confirmation when they described to Columbus the black men who traded with them.

Another important economic consideration relative to how historical African art was produced involves the form of currency used. It is imperative that one study the minting process relative to types of coins used in exchange to assess how money was controlled. Today historical African art is found in museums around the globe, especially in countries in the West. There are those who embrace these works as objects of contemplation and amusement. In certain cases, these works are used to express political bias. Viewing objects encased in glass minus context, the public can fail to link such works to a vibrant economic activity that contributed heavily to a people's gross domestic product in a particular era.

Yet another economic consideration that pertains to production of historical African art is germane to design. For any object to be perfect, it had to adhere to mathematic theories. If an object failed the mathematics test, simultaneously it failed the aesthetic test. To acquire a skill to make these objects, one had to have received some form of education. Surely Africans are not like birds that transfer nest-making skills through genes. My grandmother's experience at designing art was not transmitted genetically to her children. In fact, all of her children did not make *amacansi*.

Education served as the nucleus for making historical African art. The economic stability of a people designing such works depended on the quality of knowledge acquired in a respective academy. This kind of knowledge is scholarly. It is well known that one of the first universities in Africa was established in Mali. Thus to study art works in relation to economics makes sense. Placing the production of such works in broader contexts enables assessment of how the knowledge base of people has been and continues to be manipulated to suit the need of exploiters. Writing out of context about a subject that one does not understand, contributes to and encourages mis-education.

People need to learn that the lives of the African ancients might serve them as an example. The world is old, but the future springs from the past. Museum holdings can be utilized in a broader context as a resource to study the history of the economics of Africa. Such exploration can rescue people from current economic exploitation to which much of the world is subjected. Museum holdings also serve as a good source to provide insight about how people can coexist with nature. This can be achieved by looking at how a people used natural materials without destroying nature. Consider a headrest that I observed in a collection. Wood carvers in kwelikaMthaniya (Africa before external barbaric regulations) used dead trees to produce the headrest. No trees were cut to make these objects. Gold, silver, and copper in spears that Columbus found in America were mined in open fields. Diamonds used in necklaces were mined in rivers. Earth was not cut open, leaving large holes and tunnels excavated for gold, diamond, and other minerals.

It is not difficult for the world to learn from Africa. How is one to contribute to molding the world's economy by drawing from an African model when the image of Africans is the most consistently negatively portrayed image in the world? There are those who rise on the world stage against the shortcomings of globalization. Ancient African nations are a point of reference and model to solve current problems. In historical African art is reflected the origin of human imagination and ingenuity and the genesis of economics.

Works Cited

Browder, Anthony T. *Nile Valley Contribution to Civilization.* The Institute of Karmic Guidance: Washington, DC, 1999.

Diop, Cheikh Anta. *African Origins of Civilization: Myth or Reality.* Lawrence Hill: New York, 1974.

Van Sertima, Ivan. *Egypt: Child of Africa.* Transaction Publishers: New Brunswick, 1995.

———. *They Came Before Columbus.* Random House: New York, 1976.

Williams, Chancellor. The Destruction of Black Civilization: Issues of Race from 4500 B.C. to 2000 A.D. Third World Press: Chicago, 1974.

Literature and Film

10

Screen Jelimuso:
Julie Dash and Political Films

Sandra M. Grayson

In *A Voice from the South* (1892), Anna Julia Cooper issues a call for black people to represent people of African descent from the standpoint of black people (225). She adds, "And what is needed, perhaps, to reverse the picture of the lordly man slaying the lion, is for the lion to turn painter" (225). Unwilling to have "black lives dominated by white texts," Cooper criticized "a system of white male power" (Washington xlii). "As a literary critic, she was uncompromising in her denunciation of white control over the black image . . ." (Washington xliii). Seemingly in response to Cooper's 1892 call, Julie Dash, an award-winning black independent filmmaker, paints "life with the coloring of fiction"[1] from the perspective of a person of African descent.

Julie Dash's films can be seen as alternative visions and narratives to those perpetuated by Hollywood.[2] Her complex, multi-layered narratives focus primarily on the multiple stories black women have to tell.[3] In "Making *Daughters of the Dust*," Dash observes that one of the continuing struggles of black filmmakers is the fight against financial and social pressure to tell only one kind of story (25). She observes that African

Americans have so many stories to tell (Dash "Making *Daughters of the Dust*" 25). In a 1997 interview with Felicia R. Lee, Dash (who grew up in the Queensbridge Housing Project in Long Island City) explains that while other filmmakers focus on the inner-city projects as a subject for their films, she dreamed of more. She has refused to make a "girls in the 'hood" film, explaining that girls who live in the projects want choices in life; they want to see images of black people's important accomplishments. Dash's dreams, as represented through her films and multimedia projects, have included stories about the Gullah people in the South Carolina Sea Islands, a black woman studio executive in 1940s Hollywood, and an African American woman computer genius.[4]

Djibril Diop Mambety[5] "believed that the role of the filmmaker was that of a *griot*—more than a storyteller, the *griot* is 'a messenger of one's time, a visionary and the creator of the future'" (Grayson "Djibril Diop Mambety" 136). When describing Julie Dash, I would slightly revise Mambety's terminology by replacing the French word *griot* with the Mande term *jelimuso*.[6] Similar to the *jelimuso*, Dash (a *screen jelimuso*) is concerned with preserving and presenting history and has artistic status. As a messenger and visionary, this *screen jelimuso* (through films and multimedia projects) poses critical alternatives to mainstream cinema, uses film as both a political tool and artistic medium, as well as continues and transforms the African American oral tradition. The following analysis will focus on Julie Dash's *The Rosa Parks Story* (2002) and *Daughters of the Dust* (1991) as political films.

Based on the actual life of the social activist Rosa Parks (who approved the script and assisted in the production), the film demonstrates Julie Dash's skill in directing political films.[7] In an interview with Tony Cox (28 February 2003), Dash describes *The Rosa Parks Story*, which contains historical exegesis and a call to action, as a chance to begin a new dialogue about Rosa Parks.[8] Early in the film when only black people are present in the City Barber Shop, Raymond Parks (a black barber who later marries Rosa) recites the Paul Laurence Dunbar poem "We Wear the Mask." He juxtaposes the poem with commentary about the Scottsboro case and racism in North America, encouraging the group to contribute to the legal defense fund for the black men in the case. He also issues a call for black people to fight injustice. After hearing a customer's warning cough that serves as an announcement that the barbershop's white owner has arrived, Raymond discontinues the discussion then turns on the radio. He waits for the white owner to leave before quoting another verse from "We Wear the Mask." This scene establishes the two worlds that the black characters experience and the codes associated with each. The poem establishes a survival strategy and primary symbol that frames the story—wearing *the mask.*

The film focuses primarily on influential moments in the life of Rosa Parks prior to the 1955 Montgomery bus boycott.[9] Rosa, like Raymond, is represented as a culturally synchronized individual who (when within the white community) is forced to mask her true feelings in order to effectively function in a predominately white society that is racist and hostile toward her because she is black. Fluent in the codes associated with two cultures, she moves in and out of two worlds: one black (represented primarily by family, home, community, and the NAACP); and the other white (represented primarily by the department store, the segregated bus, the jail, and the voter registration office). In the film, dominant white culture represents the primary threat to the black characters.

Rosa Parks occasionally removes the mask in order to fight injustice. This action is exemplified in the scene in the voter registration office when she successfully challenges the white employee who repeatedly refuses to register Rosa to vote although she passes the test (and pays fees) multiple times. Her fight against discrimination is also represented in the scene where she refuses to give up her seat on the bus to a white passenger, an action which leads to the Montgomery bus boycott. The film explores the ways that racism and discrimination impacted the personal life of Rosa Parks and considers the ways she (individually, as well as in conjunction with the black community) successfully challenged discrimination and racism. *The Rosa Parks Story* represents a complex individual, who wears the mask in order to survive in a hostile society, yet removes that mask to fight against discrimination and to achieve social change.

Like *The Rosa Parks Story*, Dash's earlier film *Daughters of the Dust* is concerned with history.[10] In a 1992 interview, Dash explains that two dynamics function simultaneously in *Daughters of the Dust*: (1) a basic integrity to historical events and concerns; and (2) the freedom to romanticize history through speculative fiction, drama, and symbolism (Baker 163, 164).[11] These two dynamics serve as points of departure to discuss *Daughters of the Dust*, which is concerned with history, mythic spaces, and complex images. The film is set in 1902 on a South Carolina Sea Island on the day that some of the Peazant family members are moving to the North American mainland. In the documentary *Touching Our Own Spirit: The Making of Daughters of the Dust*, Dash explains that she saw each character in the film as representing a specific *orisha* (Yoruba deity), and she sent each actor information about the *orisha* that her/his character represents in addition to the character background sheets.[12] In the handwritten notes in the script, Nana Peazant (the leader, oldest member of the family, a former slave, and one of the narrators) is juxtaposed with Obatala.[13] The link to Obatala, the Yoruba deity responsible for creation, elevates Nana Peazant to the status of a deity, and her supernatural abilities enhance this representation. She seems to be omnipresent, transcending time and space, and has the ability to send her spirit with those who plan to relocate to the mainland. Simultaneously, her spirit will remain on the island where she physically exists. That Nana is a mediator between temporal and spiritual realms is exemplified in the graveyard scene when she communicates with the dead; she visits the graveyard everyday. In traditional Kongo belief, the cemetery is a door (*mwelo*) between two worlds, a "threshold" marking the line between two worlds (the living and the dead) circumscribed by the cosmic journey of the sun (Thompson 27). In the Kongo, "the graves were the principal medium through which the living communicated with the dead" (Hilton 11). In *Daughters of the Dust*, the ancestors guide Unborn Child into the world of the living in response to Nana's prayer.

In addition, Nana Peazant chronicles, interprets, and analyzes Peazant family history, as well as events during the slave era. In a voice-over, she explains that like the African *griot* the elders in the slave community would memorize family records, including all the births, deaths, and marriages. During the slave era in North America, the elders would also recall when family members were sold. In another scene, she explains to the family that when she was a child her mother gave her a lock of her hair before her mother was sold away. In order to create a bond between the Peazants who stay on the Sea Island and those who move North, Nana Peazant creates a "hand" that includes her hair and that of her mother. Nana tries to resolve rifts among family members, as well as religious differences, through the ritual of spirit regeneration that she leads for the family members. She ties the "hand" she creates to Viola's Bible, representing the old gods with new names, Nana Peazant, the ancestors, and the Igbos (Dash "The Script" 158-159). The ceremony is intended to give the family strength and to create a bond between them that transcends time and space (Dash "The Script" 160). Nana Peazant preserves social customs and values and is knowledgeable and instructive about proper behavior. This is exemplified in the graveyard scene when she explains to Eli that the living must communicate with the ancestors and that the ancestors watch over the living family members. She also explains to Eli that he does not own his wife Eula; she married him, and he needs to call on their ancestors to help and to guide him. Nana explains that she is trying to teach them how to touch their spirits and how to survive in the North. In a later scene, she reminds Haagar, who married into the family and does not respect the traditional beliefs, that the bottle tree located near the house reminds the family members of the ancestors and reminds each family member to appreciate loved ones. Also, Nana Peazant can read and interpret signs (such as the great wind that announces Unborn Child's arrival—Nana can sense Unborn Child's presence).

Associating Nana Peazant with Obatala and representing her as a leader in *Daughters of the Dust* can be seen as a metaphor for traditional Yoruba culture. In the Oyo Empire[14] (created by the Yoruba), as in some other ancient African nations including the Asante Empire and Kush, some women exercised power over the general public. These ancient African nations can be seen as historical sites of black women's political power. In Yorubaland, some women held (and in some cases still hold) important political positions including *alaafin*[15] (for example, a woman, one of Oduduwa's[16] daughters, founded and ruled the state of Ketu); *iyalode* (a person in charge of public affairs and the markets); *baale* (village head); and the chieftaincy titles *arise* and *lobun* (Oyewumi 96, 98, 108-109). Although there are no female kings today, "the decision by women not to compete with the men for the kingship was of their own volition, not imposed by the men" (Lawal 267). Women are also significant in Yoruba religious beliefs and are linked to supernatural power.

Among the Asante "that some female authority figures should exercise their powers over men as well as women—over the entire populace—was entirely acceptable" (Farrar 591). According to Asante cosmogony and the *Ashanti Stool Histories*, women founded the various Asante clans that became the Asante states that later united to form the Asante Empire. The Asante Empire "commanded the politics and trade of central Guinea for nearly two centuries . . . Their capital at Kumasi grew into a large and bustling center of political, commercial, intellectual, and religious life" (Davidson 238). By 1661 the Asante states began to combine, by 1750 Asante predominated in central Guinea, and by 1775 the Asante Empire became very powerful (Davidson 306). As was the case with the Oyo Empire, in the Asante nation some women had significant political roles. Sweetman observes:

> The importance of women in Asante government is shown by the fact that a new asantehene [Asante king] was selected by the queen mother, in consultation with certain advisors, from among her daughter's sons or her daughter's daughter's sons. From earliest times, in different Akan

states, the queen mother had ruled when the king died or was deposed and no successor had been appointed. (85)

Furthermore, the Akan *ohemmaa* (female ruler) "holds her title because of her seniority in the royal matrilineage and not because of any relation to a particular male" (Farrar 585).[17] The *ohemmaa* is still significant in Asante culture today, although she does not hold the same political power as she did in the Asante Empire (Grayson *Symbolizing the Past* 34-35). Additional examples of female African leaders ruling nations independent of men and exercising direct authority include the ruler of the ancient Ethiopian Empire Makeda (whose father in 1005 BC "appointed her to succeed him")[18] and the sovereign Kentakes[19] of ancient Kush, including Shenakdakhete, Amanirenas, Amanishakhete, Nawidemak, and Maleqereabar (William and Finch 17 and 30).

The governments of the Oyo Empire, Asante Empire, and Kush included some black women who wielded full political power (and in all three of these nations, a deceased king could be succeeded by a female or male offspring or other female or male relative).[20] However, as Tarikhu Farrar cautions,

[One] should be careful about dealing with women as a monolithic category in the various societies . . . It is quite conceivable that, in any given society, women who figured among the commonfolk—the great majority of women in any society—could have been relatively powerless, in society in general and in the family organization, while royal and aristocratic women in this very same society, on the other hand, were in possession of considerable political authority, social status, and substantial power within the family structure. (582)

The status of royal and aristocratic women does not necessarily reflect that of women in general or the prevailing gender relations in the society (Farrar 583). However, symbolic connections can be made between *Daughters of the Dust* and the historical facts that some black women did rule some African nations (independent of men), as well as held political titles (and wielded true political power) in some ancient Africa nations. The film does not attempt to provide a historical record of ancient African empires. Rather, the representation of Nana Peazant as a Yoruba deity and leader can be interpreted as a symbol of black women's political (and in some cases also supernatural) power in some traditional African nations. In addition, in *Daughters of the Dust* this metaphor represents other ways of knowing the world and functions as an icon for a location where some black women had central roles in society and could have the highest role in the government. Primarily through metaphor, the film reflects intersections between ancient African history and potential contemporary social transformation. By including Yoruba culture and religious beliefs symbolically, *Daughters of the Dust* suggests alternative possibilities for representing black women. *Daughters of the Dust* establishes a mythic universe where images of black women are central; represents black women as figures of resistance and empowerment; and links images of African American women to African deities and African female rulers.

The Rosa Parks Story and Daughters of the Dust represent complex, diverse images of black people, and the films reflect Julie Dash's artistic vision which is also political in that she uses film as a means to try and transform society. This methodology reflects the interconnectedness of artistic and social phenomena. Regarding African cinema, Mbye Cham observes,

> It is significant to stress that these filmmakers are aware of the limitations of the immediate political impact of their work . . . In this ideology of art the role of the artist is not to make the revolution but to prepare its way through clarification, analysis and exposure, to provide people with a vision and a belief that a revolution is necessary, possible and desirable. ("Film Text and Context")

Similarly, I would argue that one of the roles that Julie Dash plays as a filmmaker is to prepare the way for social change through "clarification, analysis and exposure, to provide people with a vision and a belief that a revolution is necessary, possible and desirable." In addition to being artistic, both *The Rosa Parks Story* and *Daughters of the Dust* function as calls for action—calls to revolutionize representations of black people in general, and black women specifically.

Notes

1. Cooper 188.
2. Most Hollywood films are patriarchal visions and myths that validate and reinforce white male domination. Mainstream cinema has generally represented black women as one-dimensional and de-historicized—if present at all, "black women are shown as sex objects, passive victims, and as 'other'

in relation to males (black and white) and white females" (Gibson-Hudson 43, 59). Repeatedly and consistently, Hollywood re-inscribes the hero-dominated perspective—from James Bond, Ethan Hunt, and Captain Jean Luc Picard to Indiana Jones, Eraser/John Kruger, and Neo, white men (and white boys—in *Lord of the Rings* and *Harry Potter*, for example) are positioned as saviors and protectors of individuals, communities, even the universe. These patriarchal visions and myths can be seen as sanctioning white male domination. Under the label "entertainment," most Hollywood films celebrate white male domination and conquest over people and places including women (through the James Bond franchise, for example); American Indians and North America (through Westerns, for example); the universe (through science fiction, for example).

3.   For a chronological list of black women filmmakers and their films see Jacqueline Bobo's "Black Women's Films: Genesis of a Tradition;" the documentary *Sisters in Cinema* (Yvonne Welbon); and Welbon's website *www.sistersincinema.*

4.   Dash was part of Los Angeles School, "a cultural movement in Black independent filmmaking" that can "be viewed as the filmic avant-garde of the 1970s" (Masilela 22). The historical moment of the Los Angeles School spanned from 1967 to 1982 (Masilela 22). Others in the group, which is also referred to as the "LA rebellion" and the "Black insurgents at UCLA" (Bambara 119) include: Haile Gerima, Charles Burnett, Ben Caldwell, and Barbara McCullough. Unlike filmmakers utilizing the conventions and formulas associated with "classic" Hollywood cinema, Dash conceptualizes her projects differently by posing critical alternatives to, representing alternative worldviews from, and challenging mainstream cinema. A list of Dash's extensive filmography and awards is included on her website (www.geechee.tv).

5.   Djibril Diop Mambety (1945-1998) was born in Dakar, Senegal. His films include: *Contras City (A City of Contrasts*, 1969); *Badou Boy*, 1970; *Touki Bouki (The Hyena's Journey*, 1973); *Hyenes (Hyenas*, 1992); *Le Franc (The Franc*, 1994); and *La Petite Vendeuse de Soleil (The Little Girl Who Sold the Sun*, 1999).

6.   *Jelimuso*, a term used primarily in Mande traditions in West Africa, refers to a female hereditary professional historian and musician who preserves and presents history through the oral tradition. pl: *jelimusow*.

7.   *The Rosa Parks Story* originally aired on CBS in North America on 24 February 2002.

8.   In that same interview, Dash recalls that Angela Bassett (one of the executive producers and stars of *The Rosa Parks Story*) called her and requested that Dash work with her on the project and that she was pleased to work with Bassett, as well as the additional people involved with the film. In a 2002 interview, Bassett credits Dash for her skill in capturing ideal pacing and

tone and for her artistic vision (Holmes "An Actress Gets to Portray an Icon").

9. Through this bus boycott, which began in December 1955 and lasted one year, black people in Montgomery, Alabama protested racially segregated seating on city buses. This boycott led to the 1956 Supreme Court decision that declared that segregated seating on buses is unconstitutional.

10. In December 2004, the Library of Congress added *Daughters of the Dust* to the National Film Registry.

11. Although generally not categorized as speculative fiction, *Daughters of the Dust* can be placed within that genre. Speculative fiction narratives include those that "contradict some known or supposed law of nature" and those "that take place in a setting contrary to known reality" (Card 17-18). The film incorporates such features. In *Daughters of the Dust* an unborn child leaves her mother's womb and influences events in 1902, and a character (Eli) walks on water. *Daughters of the Dust* can be seen as an "alternate world" narrative in that the film is set in the historical past, but certain details in the narrative contradict known facts of history. For example, Bilal Muhammed is placed in 1902, although (as Dash acknowledges that her research revealed) the actual person lived during the 1800s, earlier than the setting of *Daughters of the Dust*. The actual individual (referred to in written records as Bilali, Bilali Muhammad, Sali-bul-Ali, or Salih Bilali) that the character Bilal Muhammed is based on was a slave in the Georgia Sea Islands. Bilali was abducted from the city of Timbo in the West African region of Futa Jallon (present-day Guinea) in the late 18th century; "after toiling on his owner's plantation for over half a century, Bilali passed away in Georgia in the mid-1860's, being an estimated 80-85 years of age. He is reported to have given his manuscript to a local writer in 1859" (Progler 9).

12. In Yoruba cosmology, Olodumare is the Supreme Being. The *orishas* are offspring of Olodumare.

13. In addition to indicating the link between Nana Peazant and Obatala, the handwritten notes in the script identify additional connections to Yoruba deities, which I refer to as "character/orisha pairs." See Sandra M. Grayson's book *Symbolizing the Past: Reading Sankofa, Daughters of the Dust, and Eve's Bayou as Histories* for detailed analysis of the following character/orisha pairs: Eula/Oya, Yellow Mary/Yemaya, Trula/Oshun, Eli/Ogun, Unborn Child/Elegba.

14. The Oyo Empire was founded sometime before 1400. Between 1610 and 1790, "Oyo became one of the largest, if not the largest, states to emerge in the southern savanna and forest regions of the Guinea coast" (Boahen 64).

15. ruler. The *alaafin* controlled central authority.

16. Oduduwa was the founding ruler of the Ife Empire in the 11th or 12th century.

17. In Akan, the word for queenmother is *ohemmaa* (female ruler), a woman who wielded true political power in ancient Ghana and could assume full control of central authority.
18. Williams and Finch note that "the various lands ascribed to [Makeda's] empire included parts of Upper Egypt, Ethiopia, parts of Arabia, Syria, Armenia, India, and the whole region between the Mediterranean and the Erythraean Sea" (17).
19. The "Kentake" was a royal institution well established in Kush (Williams and Finch 20).
20. As a starting place for more information about women's significant roles in the government and military in ancient African nations, see Farrar, "The Queen Mother, Matriarchy, and the Question of Female Political Authority in Precolonial West African Monarchy;" Kolawole, *Womanism and African Consciousness*; Oyewumi, *The Invention of Women*; Sweetman, *Women Leaders in African History*; and Van Sertima, *Black Women in Antiquity*.

Works Cited

Abimbola, Adetokunbo. "Sango Images of an African Empire Builder." *Journal for the Third Millennium* 1 (Spring 1997): 21-24.

Abimbola, Wande. "Ifa as a Body of Knowledge and as an Academic Corpus." *Journal of Culture and Ideas* 1 (1983): 1-11.

———. *Ifa Divination Poetry*. New York: Nok Publishers, 1977.

———. *Ifa: An Exposition of the Ifa Literary Corpus*. Ibadan: Oxford University Press Nigeria, 1976.

———. *Sixteen Great Poems of Ifa*. Unesco, 1975.

Abiodun, Rowland. "Hidden Power: Osun, the Seventeenth Odu." *Osun Across the Waters: A Yoruba Goddess in African and the Americas*. Ed. Joseph M. Murphy and Mei-Mei Sanford. Bloomington: Indiana University Press, 2001.10-33.

Ajayi, J. F. Ade. *History of West Africa*. New York : Columbia University Press, 1976.

Baker, Houston. "Not Without My Daughters: A Conversation with Julie Dash and Houston A. Baker, Jr." *Transition* 57 (1992): 150-166).

Bambara, Toni Cade. "Reading the Signs, Empowering the Eye: *Daughters of the Dust* and the Black Independent Cinema Movement. *Black American Cinema*. Ed. Manthia Diawara. New York: Routledge, 1993. 118-144.

Boahen, Adu with Jacob F. Ade Ajayi and Michael Tidy. *Topics in West African History*. England: Longman Group Limited,1986.

Carby, Hazel V. Introduction. *The Magazine Novels of Pauline Hopkins*. New York: Oxford University Press, 1988. 441-621.

———. *Reconstructing Womanhood: The Emergence of the Afro-American Woman Novelist*. New York: Oxford University Press, 1987.

Card, Orson Scott. *How to Write Science Fiction and Fantasy*. Cincinnati: Writer's Digest Books, 1990.

Cham, Mbye. "Film Text and Context: Reweaving Africa's Social Fabric Through Its Contemporary Cinema." http://www.newsreel.org/articles/context.htm

Collins, Patricia Hill. *Black Feminist Thought: Knowledge, Consciousness, and the Politics of Empowerment*. New York: Routledge, 1991.

Cooper, Anna Julia. *A Voice From the South*. 1892. New York: Oxford University Press, 1988.

Cox, Tony. "Interview: Julie Dash on Her Nomination for a Directors Guild of America Award." Tavis Smiley (NPR). 28 February 2003. *Newspaper Source*. EBSCO. http://web.ebscohost.com.

Dash, Julie. "Making *Daughters of the Dust*." *Daughters of the Dust: The Making of an African American Women's Film*. Julie Dash. New York: The New Press, 1992. 1-26.

———. "The Script: Daughters of the Dust." *Daughters of the Dust: The Making of an African American Women's Film*. Julie Dash. New York: The New Press, 1992. 75-164.

Daughters of the Dust. Videocassette. Written and directed by Julie Dash. Geechee Girls Productions, 1991. 113 minutes.

Davidson, Basil. *A History of West Africa 1000-1800*. Essex, England: Longman Group Limited, 1977.

Davis, Angela. "Reflections on the Black Woman's Role in the Community of Slaves." *The Angela Davis Reader*. Ed. Joy James. Oxford: Blackwell Publishers Ltd., 1998. 111-128.

Davis, Zeinabu Irene. "*Daughters of the Dust*." *Black Film Review* 6.1 (1992): 12-17, 20-21.

———. "Woman with a Mission: Zeinabu Irene Davis on Filmmaking." *Hot Wire* 7 (1991): 18, 19, and 56.

Diawara, Manthia. "Black American Cinema: The New Realism." *Black American Cinema*. Ed. Manthia Diawara. New York: Routledge, 1993. 3-25.

Duran, Lucy. "Jelimusow: The Superwomen of Malian Music." *Power, Marginality, and African Oral Literature*. Ed. Graham Furniss and Liz Gunner. Cambridge: Cambridge University Press, 1995. 197-207.

Farrar, Tarikhu. "The Queen Mother, Matriarchy, and the Question of Female Political Authority in Precolonial West African Monarchy." *Journal of Black Studies* 27.5 (1997): 579-597.

Gibson-Hudson, Gloria J. "The Ties that Bind: Cinematic Representations by Black Women Filmmakers." *Black Women Film and Video Artists*. Ed. Jacqueline Bobo. New York: Routledge, 1998. 43-66.

Grayson, Sandra M. "Djibril Diop Mambety: A Retrospective." *Research in African Literature* 32.4 (2001): 136-139.

————. *Symbolizing the Past: Reading Sankofa, Daughters of the Dust, and Eve's Bayou as Histories*. Lanham, Maryland: University Press of America, 2000.

Hale, Thomas A. *Griots and Griottes: Masters of Words and Music*. Bloomington: Indiana University Press, 1998.

Harris, Kwasi. "New Images: An Interview with Julie Dash and Alile Sharon Larkin." *The Independent* (December 1986): 16-20.

Hilton, Anne. *The Kingdom of Kongo*. Oxford: Clarendon Press, 1985.

Holmes, Emory II. "An Actress Gets to Portray an Icon." *Los Angeles Times* 22 February 2002. F26.

Hooks, Bell. *Black Looks: Race and Representation*. Boston: South End Press, 1992.

Kolawole, Mary E. Modupe. *Womanism and African Consciousness*. New Jersey: Africa World Press, 1997.

Lawal, Babatunde. *The Gelede Spectacle and Social Harmony in an African Culture*. Seattle: University of Washington Press, 1996.

Lee, Felicia R. "In the Old Neighborhood with Julie Dash: Home is Where the Imagination Took Root." *New York Times* 3 December 1997. E1. LexisNexis Academic. http://web.lexis-nexis.com

Mambety, Djibril Diop with June Givanni. "African Conversations." *Sight and Sound* 5.9 (1995): 30-31.

Masilela, Ntongela. "Women Directors of the Los Angeles School." *Black Women Film & Video Artists*. Ed. Jacqueline Bobo. New York: Routledge, 1998. 21-41.

Monges, Miriam Maat-Ka-Re. *Kush, the Jewel of Nubia*. New Jersey: Africa World Press, 1997.

Oyewumi, Oyeronke. *The Invention of Women: Making an African Sense of Western Gender Discourses*. Minneapolis: University of Minnesota Press, 1997.

Progler, Yusuf. "Reading Early American Islamica: An Interpretive Translation of the 'Bilali Diary.'" *Al-Tawhid*. 16.3 (2000): 5-43.

Sisters in Cinema. Videocassette. Directed by Yvonne Welbon. 2003. 62 minutes.

Snowden, Frank M. Jr. *Before Color Prejudice: The Ancient View of Blacks*. Cambridge: Harvard University Press, 1983.

————. "The Negro in Ancient Greece." *American Anthropologist*. 50.1 (1948): 31-44.

Sweetman, David. *Women Leaders in African History*. New Hampshire: Heinemann Educational Books, Inc., 1984.

Thompson, Robert Farris. *The Four Moments of the Sun: Kongo Art in Two Worlds*. Connecticut: Eastern Press, 1981.

Touching Our Own Spirit: The Making of Daughters of the Dust. DVD. Written and directed by Julie Dash. Kino International Corp., 1999.

Van Sertima, Ivan, ed. *Black Women in Antiquity*. London: Transaction Publishers, 1992.

Washington, Mary Helen. Introduction. *A Voice From the South*. By Anna Julia Cooper. 1892. New York: Oxford University Press, 1988. xxvii-liv.

Wilks, Ivor. "Salih Bilali of Massina." *Africa Remembered: Narratives by West Africans from the Era of the Slave Trade*. Ed. Philip D. Curtin. Madison: University of Wisconsin Press, 1967. 145-151.

Williams, Larry and Charles S. Finch. "The Great Queens of Ethiopia." *Black Women in Antiquity*. Ed. Ivan Van Sertima. London: Transaction Publishers, 1992. 12-35.

11

Recalling Sovereign Kentakes:
Pauline Hopkins' *Of One Blood*

Sandra M. Grayson

History and mythic spaces intersect in Pauline Hopkins' *Of One Blood: Or, The Hidden Self* (1902-1903), a novel which represents images of African American women that are linked (through direct reference or symbolism) to female rulers of ancient African nations. In the context of this analysis, the phrase *mythic space* can be defined as a symbolic realm where the seemingly impossible is possible and where alternative ways of representing and knowing the world are explored. In *Of One Blood*, the ancient civilization of Kush and the royal institution of the Kentake survive into the 20th century.

Pauline Hopkins is probably the first African American woman to link literary images of a black woman in North America and a female African ruler. In *Of One Blood*,[1] this link is established through Mira, the protagonist's mother, who has supernatural powers and could foretell the future. Mira, an enslaved African, is a descendant of the female and male monarchs of ancient Kush, a rich and powerful ancient African nation also referred to as Ethiopia or ancient Nubia. Mira returns to the world of the living as a spirit, visits her children, and tries to guide them. The protagonist (Reuel Briggs) inherits his mysticism and supernatural powers from Mira. The narrator observes that the mystic within Reuel reflects Ethiopia's power (558). In *Of One Blood*, Kush is referred to as Ethiopia and the Kushites are referred to as Ethiopians. The Egyptian name for ancient Nubia was "Kush," while the Greeks referred to Kush as "Ethiopia" and the Kushites as "Ethiopians," a name which derives from the Greek word "Aethiopia" (Snowden *Before Color Prejudice* 3). Historically, Kush was an advanced, ancient black African civilization that rivaled ancient Egypt.[2]

Although the novel has several subplots, the main storyline focuses on Reuel's physical and spiritual journey and his eventual acceptance of his racial identity. Regarding the novel's narrative conventions, Hazel Carby observes,

> Popular conventions of narrative fiction structure the revelations of kinship in the novel. Babies are switched at birth, and the history of kinship between characters is confirmed by magical signs . . . But the impossibility of resolving *Of One Blood* within the framework of popular formulas dominates the conclusion. The social relations of the institution of slavery determine the relationships of contemporary society, and Hopkins offers no possibility that these contradictions can be resolved within the boundaries of the United States. (Carby xlvii)

When the novel opens, Reuel Briggs is passing for white and living in Boston. He later accepts an offer to serve as the medical doctor for an expedition in Africa. The members of the expedition are searching for the site of the ancient Ethiopian state of Meroe. While on the expedition, Reuel inadvertently finds the entrance to the hidden Ethiopian city of Telassar, and the leaders take him to the interior of the city. Ai, a prime minister in the city, explains that the Ethiopians in the hidden city of Telassar are a remarkable people who are governed by a female monarch (named Candace[3]) and a council of twenty-five sages (561).

According to the narrator in *Of One Blood*, the tradition among those who had known Reuel in childhood is that he is descended from African kings (558). However, the internal textual evidence actually suggests that Reuel, his mother Mira (from whom he inherits his supernatural powers), sister Dianthe, and brother Aubrey descended from female and male African monarchs, not exclusively male rulers (555, 561). Since a female monarch governs the direct descendants of the Kushites (who now reside in the hidden city Telassar), it is reasonable to speculate that female rulers (at least periodically) also governed the ancient Kushites. According to Ai, after Ergamenes[4] arrives, the current female monarch plans to inaugurate a reign of kings (561), suggesting that the tradition has been for

African women to rule the nation. Although the reason for the transition to a government ruled exclusively by men is not articulated in the novel, the novel does suggest that Candace's decision to implement the change was of her own volition, not imposed by the men.

In ancient Africa, some women ruled nations, were excellent militarists, and lead their armies into battle.[5] Examples of female African leaders ruling nations independent of men and exercising direct authority include the ruler of the ancient Ethiopian Empire Makeda (whose father in 1005 BC "appointed her to succeed him")[6] and the sovereign Kentakes of ancient Kush, including Shenakdakhete, Amanirenas, Amanishakhete, Nawidemak, and Maleqereabar (Williams and Finch 17 and 30). The "Kentake" was a royal institution well established in Kush (Williams and Finch 20).

[The] husbands [of the female rulers] were consorts to them. These queens ran the civil administration, led armies against military foes, promoted long-distance commerce and diplomatic relations, and engaged in massive building programs. In every way, they exercised the full prerogatives and powers of rulership. Such independent female rulers are found throughout Africa in time and space. (Williams and Finch 15-16)

In the history of Kush, as in *Of One Blood*, there were some African women monarchs. However, the novel's ties to African history are transformed, and the depiction of the historical existence of female rulers in Kush seems to be a point of reference to provide background information for this science fiction-style alternative history novel, where in the hidden city Telassar the inhabitants of Meroe (who are secluded from the outside world) wait for the coming of the person who will restore ancient glory to Kush (546-547). Reuel Briggs is the person for whom they have been waiting; the final proof of his identity is the birthmark (a black lotus-lily) on his chest. Near the end of the novel, Queen Candace willingly marries Reuel and gives him control of the government.

The representation of Kush in *Of One Blood* can be seen as a metaphor for a historical site of black women's political power. Additional examples of female rulers of traditional African nations include Queen Amina of Zaria (15th or 16th century) and Queen Nzinga of Angola (1581-1663). Queen Amina "is said to have created the only Hausa empire and to have led into battle a fierce army of horsemen" (Sweetman 22). In addition to being the ruler of Angola, Queen Nzinga was the "military strategist and although past sixty led her warriors herself" (Sweetman 46). Between "1630 and 1635 [Queen Nzinga] built up her new country" (Sweetman 43).

The governments of Kush and some other African nations included black women who wielded full political power (and a deceased king could be succeeded by a female or male offspring or other female or male relative), but as Tarikhu Farrar explains the status of royal and aristocratic women does not necessarily reflect that of women in general or the prevailing gender relations in the society (Farrar 583). However, symbolic connections can be made between *Of One Blood* and the historical fact that some black women ruled some ancient African nations. In *Of One Blood*, ancient Kush can be seen as a symbol of black women's political power in some ancient African nations, as well as a source of supernatural power. The distinct mythic universe created in the novel is a space where ancient Kush is recalled, providing a foundation and point of departure to develop the speculative fiction narrative. Through a mythohistory and a mythic universe, *Of One Blood* creates and explores diverse images of black people. The artistic vision is also political in that Pauline Hopkins used literature as a means to try and transform society, a methodology that reflects the interconnectedness of artistic and social phenomena.

Notes

1. Hopkins' novel *Of One Blood* originally appeared serially in *Colored American Magazine* (volume 6, numbers 1-11, November-December 1902 and January-November 1903).
2. Ethiopians figure prominently in Greek mythology, literature, and society. In the *Iliad*, for example, Ethiopians are described as loyal and lordly (91). In both the *Iliad* (91, 566) and the *Odyssey* (78, 161), the Greek gods enjoy visiting their Ethiopian *friends* where they share in *sacred* feasts. In Greek mythology, Andromeda is an Ethiopian princess (daughter of the Ethiopian King Kepheus and Queen Kassiepeia), who Perseus rescues from a monster. Perseus then marries Andromeda. As Williams and Finch explain, "Andromeda, the Ethiopian princess and Perseus's queen, figures as the founding ancestress of Mycenae, pointing to an early Ethiopian antecedent of Greek civilization, rendered mythologically" (14-15). In "The Negro in Ancient Greece," Frank M. Snowden observes that

> several authors give rather definite information as to what the Greeks thought of the Negro in his native land. Diodorus spoke highly of the civilized Ethiopians who inhabited Meroe and the land adjoining Egypt. He regarded the Ethiopians

as the first people to worship the gods, and most Egyptian institutions as deriva-
tives of their civilization. Lucian records that the Ethiopians were the first to de-
liver the doctrines of astrology to men and that their reputation for wisdom was
great. . . . Quintus of Smyrna . . . records that the Ethiopians at Troy excelled in
battle. Negroes on the coinage of Phocis, Delphi, Lesbos, and Athens point to the
existence of a tradition which honored some Negro hero, whether it was Delphos,
as some have maintained, or some unknown black hero. (37)

3. "Candace" or "Kandake" is actually the title for (not the name of) a female
   ruler of Kush. Williams and Finch note that the word "Candace" is a "Latini-
   zation of the word 'Kantake'" (20).
4. It is later established that Reuel is Ergamenes.
5. As a starting place for further discussion about black women in ancient African nations see Farrar, "The Queen Mother, Matriarchy, and the Question of
   Female Political Authority in Precolonial West African Monarchy;" Kolawole, *Womanism and African Consciousness*; Oyewumi, *The Invention of
   Women*; Sweetman, *Women Leaders in African History*; and Van Sertima,
   Black Women in Antiquity.
6. Williams and Finch note that "the various lands ascribed to [Makeda's] empire included parts of Upper Egypt, Ethiopia, parts of Arabia, Syria, Armenia, India, and the whole region between the Mediterranean and the Erythraean Sea" (17).

Works Cited

Ajayi, J. F. Ade. *History of West Africa*. New York : Columbia University Press,
1976.

Boahen, Adu. *Topics in West African History*. England: Longman Limited
Group, 1986.

Carby, Hazel V. Introduction. *The Magazine Novels of Pauline Hopkins*. New
York: Oxford University Press, 1988. 441-621.

Farrar, Tarikhu. "The Queen Mother, Matriarchy, and the Question of Female
Political Authority in Precolonial West African Monarchy." *Journal of Black
Studies* 27.5 (1997): 579-597.

Homer. *The Iliad*. Translated by Robert Fagles. New York: Penguin Books,
1990.

———. *The Odyssey*. Translated by Robert Fagles. New York: Penguin Books,
1996.

Hopkins, Pauline. *Of One Blood: Or, the Hidden Self. The Magazine Novels of
Pauline Hopkins*. General Ed. Henry Louis Gates, Jr. New York: Oxford
University Press, 1988. 441-621.

Kolawole, Mary E. Modupe. *Womanism and African Consciousness*. New Jersey: Africa World Press, 1997.

Monges, Miriam Maat-Ka-Re. *Kush, the Jewel of Nubia.* New Jersey: Africa World Press, 1997.

Oyewumi, Oyeronke. *The Invention of Women: Making an African Sense of Western Gender Discourses.* Minneapolis: University of Minnesota Press, 1997.

Snowden, Frank M. Jr. *Before Color Prejudice: The Ancient View of Blacks.* Cambridge: Harvard University Press, 1983.

———. "The Negro in Ancient Greece." *American Anthropologist* 50.1 (1948): 31-44.

Sweetman, David. *Women Leaders in African History.* New Hampshire: Heinemann Educational Books, Inc., 1984.

Van Sertima, Ivan, ed. *Black Women in Antiquity.* London: Transaction Publishers.

Williams, Larry and Charles S. Finch. "The Great Queens of Ethiopia." *Black Women in Antiquity.* Ed. Ivan Van Sertima. London: Transaction Publishers, 1992. 12-35.

12

An Interview with
Akachi Adimora-Ezeigbo

Muyiwa Falaiye and Sandra M. Grayson

FALAIYE and GRAYSON: What challenges have you experienced as a
woman writer?

ADIMORA-EZEIGBO: Though I have not had much difficulty in getting my books published, I have had other issues to contend with. One
of them is the fact that the works of women writers are not highly
valued in Nigeria. Consequently, very few critics or literary journal-
ists (who are mostly male) bother to discuss or evaluate or assess
women authored works. The disadvantage this gives to my works is
that they are rarely talked about or discussed as they really should be.
There is an unfortunate culture of silence surrounding these books
and books by other women writers in Africa.

FALAIYE and GRAYSON: How did you start writing?

ADIMORA-EZEIGBO: I started writing when I was a teenager. I attended an excellent mission school in Port Harcourt (Nigeria) where
the missionary teachers exposed us to English literature. I read a lot of
books in our well-stocked library. I actually started writing while I

was in secondary school. I used to draw pictures (cartoons) and put words in each picture. Then I gave them to my younger siblings to read. In my last year in the secondary school (form 5), I became the president of the dramatic society. It was at this point that I wrote my first play for the dramatic society. However, the play was not staged. I cannot now recall the title of the play. I did not preserve the manuscript of the play. With the benefit of hindsight now, I wish I did. During the Nigerian Civil War (1967-1970), I wrote a novel. The manuscript of that novel entitled *Tainted Custom* is still with me, 25 years or so after it was first written. I always had (and still have) a passion to write. My late father encouraged me—that is why I honor him by retaining my maiden name in the byline of my literary works. The name "Adimora" is my father's name; it appears in virtually all of my creative writings.

FALAIYE and GRAYSON: What do you hope people will learn from your works?

ADIMORA-EZEIGBO: I write about the history of my people; I write about the relationship between men and women; and about women empowerment and women's experiences in our male-dominated society. I also write about political and religious conflicts in my society. All these issues are relevant to my people's lives, and I hope my works will help to give insight to the gender-related traumas women go through in order to change their situation. I also hope my readers will get to know more about our history by reading my works so that they learn from the mistakes of the past in order to bring about social and political change. I want people to learn about the impact of negative traditions. My writings discuss issues such as the ill treatment of widows, the marginalization of female children, and the disinheriting of women.

FALAIYE and GRAYSON: How has your writing changed from your first publication to your most recent book?

ADIMORA-EZEIGBO: I started with writing short stories and children's books. My first four published books were two collections of short stories and two children's books. Later, I ventured into writing novels. My publisher observed that my strength is in creating strong female characters, especially in traditional society. He advised me to write a novel exploring such characters. This I did. The result was the novel entitled *The Last of the Strong Ones*. Later, I wrote a trilogy by adding two more novels—*House of Symbols* (2001) and *Children of the Eagle* (2002) to complement my first novel. In 2003, I wrote a book for children, *Alani the Trouble Maker and Other Stories*—a collection of four stories for children between the ages of 8-12 years old.

FALAIYE and GRAYSON: In addition to being a writer, you are Professor and former Chair of the Department of English at the University of Lagos. How did these roles intersect?

ADIMORA-EZEIGBO: Both roles complement each other very well. As an academic and literary critic, I feel my creative writing has been richer. My life as a professional critic and academic has impacted positively on my craft as a writer. The only problem is that my work as an academic and as a university administrator robed me of the precious time I could otherwise have devoted to my writing. Consequently, I did not complete much writing or research since 2002 when I served as Chair of the Department of English.

FALAIYE and GRAYSON: What opportunities have you had to mentor other writers and professors?

ADIMORA-EZEIGBO: Plenty of opportunities to do both. I am a member of two professional writing organizations in Nigeria—Association of Nigerian Authors (ANA) and Women Writers Association of Nigeria (WRITA). I served as the ANA National Treasurer from 1995-1997. From 1997-2000, I have served as the first National Vice President of WRITA. Since 2002, I have served as the National Financial Secretary of WRITA. In these two organizations, I have encouraged and advised younger writers, as well as read and edited their works. I have also commented on their works at our monthly readings where writers read from their work in progress. In the academy, I have successfully supervised doctoral dissertations and continue to work with doctoral candidates.

FALAIYE and GRAYSON: What are your plans for future literary projects?

ADIMORA-EZEIGBO: I intend to write more, engage in additional research, and publish more books. I have sufficient material for writing more novels and short stories. I also have quite a number of children's books planned.

FALAIYE and GRAYSON: How can people purchase copies of your books?

ADIMORA-EZEIGBO: Some of my books can be purchased online, including *Rhythms of Life, Rituals and Departures, The Buried Treasure*, and *The Prize*. The rest of my books can be purchased from bookstores in Nigeria, such as University of Lagos Bookstore, University of Ibadan Bookstore, and Glendora Bookstore.

FALAIYE and GRAYSON: What are your thoughts on collaborative projects between English Departments in Africa and in the United States?

ADIMORA-EZEIGBO: I welcome the idea of collaborative projects whole heartedly. In fact my university is currently exploring such projects. Dr. Oye Ibidapo-Obe's (President of the University of Lagos) visit to the United States in 2004 is connected with such a noble and potentially enriching idea. Previously, visitors from two American Universities came to the University of Lagos to explore ways they can establish links with us. I am deeply interested in forging such collaborations.

FALAIYE and GRAYSON: What advice would you give to students who want to become writers and/or professors?

ADIMORA-EZEIGBO: I would advise them to work hard and persistently. Those who want to be writers must learn not to rush through the process; they should revisit their manuscripts and rework and improve the text as often as possible. Those who aspire to be professors must develop good writing skills as well. They must be ready to complete thorough research and publish the results of their research. The bottom line is hard work. There is no substitute for hard work.

Selected Publications by Akachi Adimora-Ezeigbo

Alani the Troublemaker and Other Stories. Lagos: Literamed Publications, 2003.

Asa and the River Goddess. Lagos: Literamed Publications, 2003.

The Buried Treasure. Oxford: Heinemann, 1994.

Children of the Eagle. Lagos: Vista Books, 2002.

A Companion to the Novel. Lagos: Vista Books, 1998.

Echoes in the Mind. Lagos: Foundation Publishers, 1994.

Fact and Fiction in the Literature of the Nigerian Civil War. Lagos: Unity Publishing and Research Company, 1992.

Gender Issues in Nigeria: A Feminine Perspective. Lagos: Vista Books, 1996.

Hazina Iliyojikwa. Oxford: Heinemann, 1996.

House of Symbols. Lagos: Oracle Books Limited, 2001.

The Last of the Strong Ones. Lagos: Vista Books, 1996.

The Prize. Oxford: Heinemann, 1994.

Rhythms of Life. London: Karnak House, 1992.

Rituals and Departures. London: Karnak House, 1996.

13

Pauline Hopkins and Social Justice

Joy Myree-Mainor

During the post-reconstruction period in the United States, racist whites increasingly used lynching, disenfranchisement, and the sexual exploitation of black women in their attempts to control black labor and maintain domination of recently emancipated blacks. At the turn of the 19th century, black women writers generated a body of cultural work including novels, plays, essays, and speeches to address these increasingly threatening waves of anti-black violence. These activists' oral and written works addressed the waves of violence and lack of equal rights, often recording the violent acts against and widespread disenfranchisement of black citizens across the nation. Overall, these activists sought both to challenge racist thought and practice and to educate and "uplift" the black majority who struggled to achieve political, economic, and social enfranchisement amidst a backlash of white racism.

Pauline Hopkins, especially in her first novel *Contending Forces* (1900), provides an exemplary model of activism for social justice because her writings specifically challenge racism. Furthermore, her methodology for attacking racism remains relevant in contemporary North American society since her approach uncovers the ideological myths that support and promote anti-black violence. Hopkins found that during post-reconstruction the impetus behind the increased violence against blacks was mainly whites' attempts to control black social, political, and economic progress. Hopkins remained a forerunner in promoting the need to uncover the systematic nature of racism, and *Contending Forces* provides a cogent analysis of how whites used myths about blacks to jus-tify the crimes of whites—the continued lynching of black men and rape and sexual exploitation of black women. Moreover, Hopkins exposed the double bind of the black woman who is twice victimized by race and gender.

Contending Forces set the tone for Hopkins' later work. In her novels and short fiction, she uses characters and situations to reflect the historical circumstances of black and white relations of her time, as well as the history of slavery that informed the racist practices of whites and the disenfranchised status of most blacks. In recreating these situations, Hopkins clearly subverts racist ideologies and exposes the barbaric acts of whites, placing the blame on whites' racist beliefs and actions. According to Hazel Carby, in Hopkins' "fictional history, the degradation of a race was not the result of degeneration through amalgamation but a consequence of an abuse of power; it was the use of brutality against a subordinate group that was defined as and equated with savagery" (Carby 134). Hopkins' fiction challenges accepted racist theory that justified the exploitation of blacks (Carby 134).

Hopkins begins *Contending Forces* with a situation that exemplifies her commitment to subverting racist ideology. Specifically, in the begin-ning of the novel, the ambiguity of the color line is exposed. The novel opens with a narrative about an apparently white slaveholding family (the Montforts) who become victims of rumors that identify the family as having black blood. Grace Montfort, the mother and wife, is eventually attacked (symbolically raped and whipped) when rumors began to circu-late about her having a strain of "Negro" blood. Her husband is killed and her children sold into slavery. The first 80 pages of the novel deal with the Montfort's demise as the family moves from the West Indies to North Carolina in the 18th century. The second (and the main) story, is set at the end of the 19th century and surrounds the lives of the families born to the heirs of the Montfort family, the descendents of Jessie and William. The heirs of Jessie (who escapes slavery, runs North, and is absorbed into the black community) take the name "Smith." The Smiths are later reunited with the descendents of William who had been bought by an Englishman and lived free in England. The novel centers on the lives of the Smith family, headed by "Ma" Smith, who runs a boarding house in Boston. The heroine of the novel, Sappho Clark (a new boarder in the Smith house), attracts the attention of Jessie's great grandchild, Will Smith. However, Sappho has a secret she keeps guarded—she was raped and gave birth to a child who was the product the rape.

The Montforts' story introduces the connections between white slave owners and their future black descendents. Hazel Carby suggests that Hopkins' characters were created not as holistic individuals but as the terrain on which the consequences of her authorial interpretation of history were worked through, making the whole Smith family the bearers of the history of colonization (142). By further creating characters whose racial identities are ambiguously assigned, Hopkins also underscores the idea that the violence perpetuated against blacks has the possibility of harming whites. In fact, the interconnection between the Montforts and the Smith family works to subvert beliefs in any pure racial origins. The novel culminates in events resulting from a series of public meetings held to protest the rise in lynching and rape in the South. At the final public meeting, Sappho's secret becomes apparent to the villainous John Langley who attempts to blackmail Sappho into becoming his mistress. The novel's conclusion suggests the need for reparations for slavery. In Hopkins' fictional world, a debt needed to be paid on two levels: the debt that accrued with the family history of the Monforts, and by extension, all descendents of enslaved blacks (Carby 136).

Hopkins' fiction also emphasizes the main origins of the mulatto class—white men's rape of black women. Hopkins uses the women's Sewing Circle to indict white male sexual assaults against black women and to advocate for a redefinition of black womanhood. In this section of the novel, a group of women meet in "Ma" Smith's parlor for the purpose of fundraising activities for their church. This meeting is symbolic of the growing numbers of black women's club activity (which by 1890, with the formation of the National Association for the Advancement of Colored Women, allowed for black women's issues to have a national forum). Hopkins and her contemporaries challenged the ubiquitous stereotype of the immoral black woman by using forums made available through the black women's club movement. Hopkins uses the voices of black women to insist that, like Harriet Jacobs, black women should not be held accountable for "sins" committed through being victimized by white male rapists. For instance, during the Sewing Circle's meeting, Sappho, who has been raped, asks if the members of the group think that God will hold black women responsible for being sexually assaulted (149). Mrs. Willis, the novel's model black woman activist, responds that she believes that black women are not to blame; the white rapist will be punished and the sin is his (149-150). In the novel, the standards of the virtuous woman are revised when Sappho reclaims her child and marries her love interest, Will Smith (Tate 175). As Claudia Tate argues, "The de-centering of the father's law in the Smith household also permits the hero Will to disregard the patriarchal code for premarital virginity" (Tate 175). As a result of Sappho's character marrying and apparently prospering, the novel both redefines notions of a virtuous woman and makes Will a more equitable partner, who may be husband as partner, not father.

Sappho's story connects the rape of black women and lynching of black men when her past history is revealed during a meeting of the male counterpart to the Sewing Circle, the American Colored League. The purpose of the meeting is the black community's response to continued lynching and rape committed against black people in the South. *Contending Forces* demonstrates "that the political issue behind the violence of lynching was not the threat of black sexuality, but the potential power of the black vote" (Carby 139). Will Smith emphasizes the connections between rape and lynching and white violence when he explains that (like in Sappho's case) usually the white man has raped a black woman. He adds that whites shoot and/or lynch black people for any number of excuses, including voting and accumulating property, and if black people defend themselves the government calls in the Federal troops (271).

This fictional representation of terrorism against blacks challenges existing beliefs about the myth of black criminality, and identifies the actual crimes whites commit against blacks. Hopkins provides an effective model of activism through her protest literature as exemplified by *Contending Forces*. Hopkins' methodology is mirrored in the contemporary works of writers such as Toni Morrison and John Edgar Wideman, and in the non-fiction work of activists such as bell hooks and Angela Davis. Like Hopkins, these writers' social activism uncovers and condemns the ideological basis on which much of white racism is based. Hopkins' strategy for seeking social justice remains important in present-day society.

Works Cited

Carby, Hazel. *Reconstructing Womanhood: The Emergence of the Afro-American Woman Novelist*. New York: Oxford University Press, 1987.

Hopkins, Pauline. *Contending Forces: A Romance Illustrative of Negro Life in North and South.* 1900. New York: Oxford University Press, 1988.

Tate, Claudia. *Domestic Allegories of Political Desire: The Black Heroine's Text at the Turn of the Century.* New York: Oxford University Press, 1992.

14

Trans-Atlantic Dimensions:
Exploring *Amistad* and *Sankofa*

Samuel Ayedime Kafewo

In the following analysis, the problematic of cinematically narrating the slavery experience will be explored through a comparative study of *Amistad* (directed by Steven Spielberg) and *Sankofa* (directed by Haile Gerima). *Amistad* is based on the actual story of 53 Africans enslaved aboard a Spanish sailing-vessel (*La Amistad*) who revolted against the crew. However, an American naval ship captured them, after which they were imprisoned at New Haven, Connecticut. After a long legal battle, the enslaved Africans regained their freedom. *Sankofa* captures the fictional story of Mona, a contemporary African American fashion model on a photo session at Elmina Castle in Ghana. While at the Castle, she is transported to the past, where she experiences life as a slave named Shola on a plantation in eighteenth century North America.

The analysis of the films will aim at a certain relationship which may be unperceived by the filmmaker, "between what he commands and what he does not command of the patterns of languages he uses . . . [it] attempts to make the not-seen accessible to sight" (Derrida 157-164). It is possible that:

A text can be read as saying something quite different from what it appears to be saying . . . it may be read as carrying a plurality of significance or as saying many different things which are fundamentally at variance with, contradictory to and subversive of what may be seen by criticism as a single "stable" meaning. Thus a text may "betray" itself. (Cuddon 72)

Monaco observes,

Two paradoxes control the politics of film: on the one hand, the form of film is revolutionary; on the other, the content is most often conservative of traditional values. Second the politics of film and the politics of "real life" are so closely intertwined that it is generally impossible to discover which is the cause and which is the effect. (219)

There is usually a dialectic between film realism and film expression: the power to mimic reality and the powers to change reality. Film, therefore, provides an effective medium to structure narrative in such a way that the system will not be threatened or in such a way that the system is thoroughly threatened.

Spielberg's *Amistad* is an *assimilation story* that celebrates and glorifies white men, many of whom were slaveholders. However, the film does not address the fact that at the time of the events in the film (and for over 20 years after the Africans in the case gained their freedom) most blacks in North America were still enslaved.

Although Spielberg described the horrendous conditions of the "middle passage," he hardly provided us with a glimpse of slavery in the U.S.: its brutal exploitative character, the slave revolts on the plantations owned by Supreme Court justices and politicians, and their suppression. Nor did he point out that the revolt aboard the *Amistad* was unusual only in the success. (Rosenthal 2)

In addition to excluding slavery in North America, the film refuses to give significant voice to the enslaved Africans. Throughout most of the film, the enslaved simply babble, while white men speak for and about them. The viewer rarely hears what the Africans are saying. Allowing the slaves to speak for themselves is crucial:

Not only the meaning of the utterance, but the very fact of its performance is of historical and social significance, as, in given circumstances, at a certain historical moment, under the conditions of a certain social situation. The very presence of the utterance is historically and socially significant. (Allen 17)

When discussing *Amistad*, Spielberg insists that the film is not about African history but American history. Does this explain why the film places so much emphasis on the courtroom and omits any plantation scenes? Perhaps plantation scenes would have exposed too much American history.

Unlike *Amistad*, Gerima's *Sankofa* is a *resistance story*. The Akan word "sankofa," the mythical and enigmatic Akan bird which is both ideologically and theoretically confounding, encapsulates a principle which portends a gateway to understanding identities in the film. Sankofa dips its beak into its tail (past), while at the same time living the present. This act suggests that one cannot live without the past. However, *Sankofa*'s trip to the past is not nostalgic or romantic (Okwori 1). The action starts at Elmina Castle, a historical site that serves as a painful reminder to people of African descent where millions of their ancestors were transported to the Americas. In the film, Mona is a professional model who comes to the Castle to complete a photo shoot. Oblivious to the historical significance of the site, she poses to satisfy a white man, who is furiously flashing his camera. The photographs will be featured in some exotic magazines. However, before the photo session is completed an old man guides Mona to her past and helps to decolonize her mind. The drums roll amidst ritual invocations. The old man, a self-appointed guardian of the Elmina Castle, is the link with the past. After he tells Mona, the white photographer, and the other tourists to leave the Castle and stop defiling it, the stage is set for a radical re-examination of the past.

The enslaved Africans in *Sankofa* are represented as complex individuals who tell their own stories. On the plantation, they either communicate directly in English or in their traditional African languages. In addition to exploring the horror of slavery and torture the enslaved Africans experienced, *Sankofa* represents the ways that the enslaved physically and psychologically resisted slavery and fought for their freedom. This representation of history recalls Graeme Turner's description of film:

Film does not reflect or even record reality; like any other medium of representation it constructs and represents pictures of reality by way of the codes, conventions, myths and ideologies of its cultures, as well as by way of the specific signifying practices of the medium . . . The film-maker, like the novelist or the storyteller, is a *bricoleur*—a sort of handyman who does the best s/he can with the materials at hand. The filmmaker uses the representational conventions and repertoires available within the culture in order to make something fresh but familiar, new but generic, individual but representative. (Turner 129)

Although both *Amistad* and *Sankofa* are about enslaved Africans during the antebellum period in North America, how the films construct "codes, conventions, myths and ideologies" reveals much about the perspective of the directors. While *Amistad* glorifies (and romanticizes) American history, *Sankofa* confronts the historical reality of slavery in antebellum North America.

Works Cited

Allen, Graham. *Intertexuality*. London: Routledge, 2002.

Derrida, J. *Of Grammatology*. Baltimore: John Hopkins University Press, 1976.

Monaco, James. *How to Read a Film: The Art, Technology, Language, History and Theory of Film and Media*. Oxford: Oxford University Press, 1982.

Okwori J. "The Sankofa Principles in Identity Construction: Festivals and Emblematic Culture among the Idoma and African Americans." Paper presented at the Institute for Advance Research in the African Humanities, Northwestern University, 15-17 May 1998.

Rosenthal, Steve. "Review of Movie *Amistad*." 1 December 1998. http://csf.colorado.edu/forums/psn/jan98/0033.html

Turner, Graeme. *Film as Social Practice*. New York: Routledge, 1998.

15

Jean Toomer's "Kabnis":
Family Portrait as Face of the South

Ronald Dorris

Born in Washington, D.C. in 1894, Jean Toomer was the grandson of P.B.S. Pinchback, lieutenant governor of Louisiana and then governor for a brief moment during Reconstruction. Toomer was cast in the literary spotlight in 1923 with the publication of his book *Cane*. Divided into three parts, the book is a composite of poems and sketches that paint secular and spiritual portraits about African American life and history. The following analysis focuses on "Kabnis," part three of *Cane* which, like much of the text, is an autobiographical account centered on Toomer's family.

After high school, Toomer sojourned across America for five years. He returned to Washington in summer 1920 and, until spring 1922, cloistered himself in an apartment to study his grandparents, whom he accepted had most influenced him. Due to ill health, his grandfather was dying. Toomer gave credit to the faith and fortitude of his grandfather and the companionship of a few friends as his sole contacts with life and his sole inspiration outside himself and his work. For Toomer, to write about his family was synonymous with writing about the South and the part that race was playing in his own development.[1] The impending death of his grandfather challenged and propelled Toomer to write about his family as a living part of the history of the South.

In addition to being challenged by the presence of his grandfather to write about the South, Toomer also was inspired by his maternal grandmother, Nina Emily Hethorn, who was from New Orleans. When Pinchback relocated from New Orleans to Washington, D.C. in 1892, Hethorn continued to keep the presence of New Orleans alive in her home. She shared many stories with Toomer about the stormy days of social and political strife. However, she also shared with him the world of Mardi Gras, myths, and legends surrounding various *krewe* that comprise carnival parades.

Cane is dedicated to Grandmother Pinchback. "Kabnis" is dedicated to Waldo Frank, an American literary figure Toomer was convinced would help him to achieve his aim as a writer. Toomer loved word-game associations, having picked up from Pinchback the art of creating names to suit the person, occasion, and mood (Kerman and Eldridge 28-29). This art is exemplified in the word "Kabnis"—K-A-N = cane and B-I-S = the nickname of Toomer's favorite maternal uncle, Bismarck Robert Pinchback. The letters K-A = an Egyptian word of the same spelling which means a presiding or second spirit present in a human or statue. Thus "Kabnis" can be interpreted as the soul of *Cane* and the soul of Bis. To showcase his family as a living part of the history of the South, Toomer wanted to create a work without apology for race. He wanted to create a work that involved examination of race as a factor in his own development and to create a distinctly American work.[2]

In one sense, "Kabnis" can be regarded as Toomer's gift to Uncle Bis for being the first major influence who helped him shape his world of ideas and imagination. "Kabnis" also stands as testimony to Bis' dreams. In Toomer's estimation, Bis was a solitary intellectual, a man of artistic pursuits, the opposite of Pinchback as a man of action and commitment. Yet for all his interest in reading and writing, Bis had not succeeded at anything noteworthy. He married at age forty-one in 1905. Until that time, he had been a strong presence in the Pinchback household but had caused as little dissention as possible. Instead, he had served to reconcile family differences until Toomer was eleven-years-old.

"Kabnis" can be assessed from a number of angles. One angle is centered on the contest between Bis and his father, Pinchback. The sketch opens with Ralph Kabnis propped in bed, trying to read himself to sleep. The cabin room is described as being spaced fantastically about this burning unsteadiness. This opening and additional scenes correspond to much that transpired in Bismarck's life. Pinchback objected to the gas lamp being burned in his son's room after ten o'clock at night. The lamp took on significant meaning in the lives of the grandfather, son, and grandson. Tying a match stick to the light fixture and attaching long black threads from the stick to reach the bed, Bis could pull the strings and dim the lights when he heard his father coming. He let his little nephew in on the secret. The boy became intrigued and delighted because he wanted his uncle to outwit his grandfather. Later Toomer wrote that he had had no notion of the deeper matters involved. In addition to rigging strings to the gas lamp switch and to covering the transom, Bis also stuffed rags under the door to his room to prevent light from escaping and cigarette smoke from trailing through the darkened house. Like Kabnis, Bis often reflected on the confinement. It seemed ironic that he, a grown man, should be subjected to so many rules in his father's house when Pinchback had attended and given smoke-filled balls to honor men all the way up the social ladder to President Grant (Kerman and Eldridge 24).

Among other considerations, the unsteadily burning oil lamp in "Kabnis" is symbolic of periodic unsteadiness that governed the Pinchback household. The whitewashed hearth and chimney in the sketch, black with sooty saw-teeth mirror, parallel the neatness yet darkness of Bis' room when Toomer was growing up. Bis' room always seemed to be in a mellow shade, wrote Toomer, a twilight, a dusk, an evening room. The patterns cast on the ceiling from the oil lamp in "Kabnis" mirror patterns on the wallpaper that once adorned Bis' room. The unpainted seasoned rosin walls in the sketch are reference to a description Toomer later painted of Bismarck's room. In contrast, Toomer wrote that the room of his younger uncle Walter was of the morning, natural, dawn.[3]

"Kabnis" is comprised of six scenes or movements. The sketch centers on a young professional from the North who has come South to teach. He joins other northern teachers in the town of Sumpter. Two of these professors are Layman and Lewis. Eventually, Kabnis is fired from his position and taken in by the blacksmith Halsey. This is the basic plot around which the story evolves. Kabnis' self-reflection enables an audience to enter his mind. He views himself as a cyclical dream that gets smashed by the squareness of the world. He would like to feel that he has come South to face this region and to become its face through what he can develop with words. The self-reflection of Ralph Kabnis coincides with a description Toomer paints of Uncle Bis in an autobiographical account (Toomer "The Early Days" 42).

Toomer finished "Kabnis" in December 1921, the day after Pinchback died. He described the sketch as semi-dramatic and would continue to refine it until he felt comfortable with a final draft. Meanwhile, a more pressing matter developed. Toomer and his youngest uncle Walter had to accompany Pinchback's body to New Orleans for burial at Metairie Cemetery. As the train sped further South, Toomer's mind was filled with the work yet remaining to bring "Kabnis" to refinement. As the train bearing Pinchback's body crossed the Louisiana line, Toomer saw reapers harvesting the cane. It was grinding season. The rhythm of the rickety wagons that sped in the fields along side the railroad track competed with the musical sound made by the train, the bent bodies of the workers rising and falling to each note. Despite toil, their whole presence seemed one of celebration of the land, celebration of the spirit of their lives in the December sun of a semi-tropical climate.

When Toomer and Walter returned to Washington, Toomer settled down and immersed himself in a period of constant writing. By October 1922, he was ready to arrange the six sketches he had worked on after "Kabnis" as part one of a book; the manufactured sketches as part two; and "Kabnis" as part three. He titled the book *Cane* and sent it to Waldo Frank, who took the manuscript to Boni and Liveright publishers. On 2 January 1923, Frank informed Toomer that Liveright had accepted *Cane* for publication. Toomer stated that the subject matter of *Cane* is mostly Negro. Additionally, *Cane* is local—the South and the Pinchback family as a living part of its history.

Toomer believed that the South, unlike the North and West, had a peasantry rooted in the soil. He also believed that the South had a basic restless maladjustment to its physical environment.[4] He felt that the rest of the country stood in sore need of the southern expression of adjustment and complexity sprinkled with stark theme of white and black races. Toomer believed that the passion of the South served as the drama of the region. He admitted that he had dreamed of writing a volume whose foundation rested on a thorough training in social and biological science. But that, said Toomer, would take years of special study and a whole reshaping of his life. Instead, he accepted that it should be possible to tone down his desire to a modest non-scholarly work that would realize those fundamentals of vision and observation pertaining to the Southern situation.[5]

Toomer sent copies of *Cane* to family members and eagerly awaited their responses. Grandmother Pinchback was pleased with publication of *Cane* because here at last was achievement on the part of her grandson. Her one regret until her death was that Pinchback had not lived to see his grandson's achievement.[6] Uncle Bis informed his nephew that he had spoken with Nina Emily Hethorne on 26 September 1923. His impression was that Hethorne seemed somewhat bewildered. She did not understand parts of *Cane*. Still she was glad that finally the book had been published and wished for it wonderful success. She also took great delight in the August and September issues of *Broom* where "Kabnis" appeared in full.[7]

After he read the book, Bis acknowledged receipt of *Cane*. He expressed that his opinion might not be useful, but he stated it anyway. Bis admitted familiarity with most scenes, characters, and general tendencies described in each sketch and story. For these reasons, he wrote, *Cane* carried less interest for him than if he had found what he thought would be a new and unknown life opened up before him. For these and other reasons, he was certain Toomer would understand better than himself, Bis did not think *Cane* would appear popular with the "brother" as a whole. He was, however, hopeful that beauty and interest in description and the strength and vigor of language in *Cane* might free other minds, as happened to him when reading the book, from preoccupation with race. Bis congratulated his nephew and hoped that he would find success in *Cane* and continue the good work. The dedication to Toomer's grandmother and the gift-note forwarded by Toomer pleased Bis immensely and touched him deeply.

During the 1920s, Jean Toomer was surrounded by death. He struggled to draw from his family as a living part of the history of the South before he lost them as an authentic source. Pinchback died the day after "Kabnis" was completed. Uncle Bis died six months after *Cane* appeared in print. Grandmother Pinchback died in September 1928. Toomer departed from a stay at York Beach, Maine to attend her funeral in Washington. Only Uncle Walter was left from the immediate circle. When Grandmother Pinchback died, the South as Toomer had come to know it was laid to rest. Toomer recorded that *Cane* was his book of death and birth. Toomer never understood why anyone expected him to write another book like *Cane*. He accepted that *Cane* was his swan song, an ending that gave rise to the birth song of a new beginning.

Notes

1. Jean Toomer Papers, Box 51, folder 1106, listed among Collection of American Literature, the Beinecke Rare Book and Manuscript Library, Yale, Library, New Haven. Subsequent references to these papers will be referred to as JTP file number: box number.
2. JTP 51:1106. This folder contains a number of drafts of "America and Problems," both handwritten and typed. Toomer's intention was to write a book about race in America. Information within these pages suggests that this work was begun before or when *Cane* was being composed.
3. JTP 12:385, Earth-Being (second draft), 184.
4. JTP 48:1008, The South in Literature, n.d. Toomer submitted this document for publication consideration to Horace Liveright. As a promotional measure, reviewers received excerpts from this essay along with copies of *Holiday* (by Waldo Frank) and *Cane*. Boni and Liveright was publisher for both books.
5. JTP 5:180, Jesse E. Moorland to Jean Toomer, 19 July 1922.
6. JTP 20:514, Book VI, 60.
7. JTP 6:213, Bismarck Pinchback to Jean Toomer, 28 September 1923.

Works Cited

Kerman, Cynthia Earl and Richard Eldridge. *The Lives of Jean Toomer: A Hunger for Wholeness*, Baton Rouge: Louisiana State University Press, 1989.
Toomer, Jean. *Cane*. 1923. New York: Liveright, 1975.
———. "The Early Days." *The Wayward and the Seeking: A Collection of Writings by Jean Toomer*. Ed. Darwin T. Turner. Washington, D.C.: Howard University Press, 1980. 28-83.

Short Stories and Poetry

16

Transfiguration

Sandra M. Grayson

"Esu in Ikoolo. Agbigbo near Ikoolo," echoes by the open window of the chamber, where the *alaafin*, ruler, of Ayanmo presides over a council meeting. A falcon lands on the widow sill and peers in the room. Paintings of the empire accentuate the vaulted ceiling of the chamber in the *aafin*, palace.

Across from the *aafin* is the *oja*, market; both are situated in the center of Ayanmo. A nucleus of economic activities, the *oja* is the crossroads where multitudes of people meet. At night, significant historical state rituals are reenacted and important occasions, including weddings, are celebrated. Usually before midnight humans turn the *oja* over to the spirits. From a reasonable distance, Alaafin Kabiyesi sees this regular assembly of the people.

Wearing the traditional wide black silk pants and golden tunic reserved for royalty, Alaafin Kabiyesi holds in her right hand a gold staff surmounted by a gold falcon, illuminated by sunlight expanding in the room. This staff is a symbol of her authority and key to indirect communication.

Alaafin Kabiyesi's eldest daughter, who will succeed her as *alaafin*, observes the proceeding. Two guards survey the room. The council consists of the Prime Minister, Finance Minister, General of the Army, and Historian.

Alaafin Kabiyesi opens the meeting by asking for reports from the council. The Prime Minister, Basorun, stands: "At dawn on my return from the university where yesterday I delivered a lecture, I saw a woman walking along a road lined with trees that offered no houses. Her long black silk dress and intricate braids complemented her ebony skin. She was beautiful. I stopped my horse and asked if she needed help. She stared at me. Leaning forward I asked, 'What is your name?' Taking a step back, she responded 'Ase.' Sliding down from the horse, I approached Ase but stopped when she began to change—two legs became four, the arms disappeared . . . where a woman once stood was a panther. The panther backed away then turned, running toward the *oja*."

"Into a panther? Are you sure of this?" the General responds as she spreads out a map of Ayanmo on a large table in the council chamber.

While Basorun watches the paper being centered, he considers the possibility that the map could actually be Ase, or she could be the table, or the General. The last possibility makes him jump when the General asks, "Where did you first see this woman?"

"What?"

The General repeats the question.

"Oh. Here. About five miles from the university." Basorun points to the approximate place on the map and gives the General drawings of the incident.

"Why would she be walking in this area? There must have been others nearby."

"No one else was in the area."

"At what point did you think something was different about this woman?"

"When she began to change. The drawings provide a better sense of what happened; she may be a threat"

"If the panther had attacked, I would agree. However, the actions of the woman and the panther suggest that they perceived you as the threat."

"I am no threat."

"To a woman walking alone in an isolated area, you may seem to be."

The *alaafin* nods in agreement at the General then looks at Akunyungba, a historian well-versed in *ese* (poems) of the divinity Ifa and the ancient scrolls. She is an influential member of the council whose wisdom is valued throughout the empire. After considering the drawings, Akunyungba begins to chant *ese* regarding Oya and her husband Sango, royalty who later became *orisha*. She concludes, "Before they were married, Sango had been told that Oya would be stronger and more successful. When they became *orisha*, Oya, who controls whirl-winds including hurricanes and tornadoes, was stronger than Sango, who controls thunder."

"What if this woman is not divine?" asks Basorun avoiding direct eye contact, which would be considered a challenge to Akunyungba's author-ity in these matters.

"What is the woman doing here?" she points to the second illustra-tion.

"Backing away."

"And here, what is the panther doing?" she points to another drawing.

"Backing away."

"A retreating panther should not be pursued," she says, picks up the drawings, and reaches these to Basorun

Alaafin Kabiyesi looks around the room for additional comments. Si-lence. Transferring the gold staff from her right hand, a movement that indicates she has made a decision, Alaafin Kabiyesi accepts the assess-ment that Ase is not a threat.

*   *   *   *

"Esu in Ikoolo. Agbigbo near Ikoolo," echoes in the vaulted ceiling of the chamber as the falcon soars across the room.

The General stands and reports that a caravan of merchants is ap-proaching from the north and recommends allowing the caravan to enter.

Nearly one thousand camels arranged in single file extend for almost three miles. In a few hours, the caravan will reach the caravansary on the main trade route about 20 miles, a one-day journey, from Ayanmo. Alaafin Kabiyesi had arranged for the construction of the caravansary, a rectangular stone building surrounding a secure courtyard, where the people and the animals of a caravan could have necessary facilities such as a well for water, rooms in which to rest and sleep, and a sheltered area for baggage. Usually, the camels were laden with goods, such as writing paper, salt, copper, and silk. Often Arabian horses were also available. Ayanmo exported such items as millet, wheat, cloth, and gold. The main currency was cowries. Organized for mutual help against the hazards of travel in the Sahara desert, members of a caravan camped throughout the empire and sold their goods at the markets with the local artisans includ-ing weavers, blacksmiths, potters, and writers. Since the population increases significantly whenever a caravan arrives, additional security measures are implemented. Generally honest in their dealings, traveling merchants are welcomed, and treated as guests.

"Esu in Ikoolo. Agbigbo near Ikoolo," echoes across the room as a woman wearing a long black silk dress, her hair intricately braided, approaches Alaafin Kabiyesi. Her words are urgent; the message seems unintelligible. After her prevision last night, she can only speak the language of prophecy. In honor and respect, she approaches the *alaafin* with the palms of her hands turned up. Alaafin Kabiyesi motions for the guards to stand down.

"Esu in Ikoolo. Agbigbo near Ikoolo," Ase repeats as Akunyungba analyzes the message.

Nearly one hour passes before Akunyungba stands and says, "In *ese Ifa*, Esu, a messenger, turned into wind to travel quickly to the ancient city of Ikoolo, where he warned the people that Agbigbo, one of their sons, was returning with a 'load of evil' on his head. If the people allowed him to put down the load, their city would be destroyed."

Alaafin Kabiyesi looks at Ase, who confirms the meaning by placing on the table an emerald shaped like a falcon. Transferring the gold staff from her right hand, the *alaafin* orders the General to send troops to search the caravan.

The caravan is still at the caravansary. Rather than find merchants, the Ayanmo army encounters invaders aligned with the *ajogun*, malevolent entities with supernatural powers. The army engages and ultimately defeats the invaders, but is unable to stop the *ajogun* approaching the empire. Sensing this invisible enemy, Ase focuses her mental powers and shields Ayanmo. Rendered powerless, the *ajogun* retreat.

*   *   *   *   *

The drum, announcing the end of battle and the beginning of a royal audience, can be heard for miles. Citizens gather outside the palace. Preceded by musicians carrying gold guitars, and followed by the council members and two guards, Alaafin Kabiyesi walks up the palace steps to the platform where she holds an audience.

The General stands before Alaafin Kabiyesi and recounts the actions of the soldiers on behalf of the empire. After witnesses confirm these accounts by beating a drum, the *alaafin* thanks the soldiers. Akunyungba stands and recounts Ase's actions on behalf of the empire. After the drumbeat, the *alaafin* thanks Ase. In honor and respect, the musicians sing praise poetry about the military and Ase.

As the wind carries the praise poetry, Ase walks up the palace steps, breathes the fresh air of Ayanmo, transforms into a falcon, and ascends into the sky.

17

Silent Steps
(for Funmilayo Ransome-Kuti)

Chimalum Nwankwo

1

Elephant country pounds the earth
And there are tremors on all shores

The oceans snarl with lips of death
And in froth and in wrath furling waves

Heat compels the trembling mountain
The fiery breath of stoppered places

Nothing on earth speaks of the molten fires
Silent in wait in the belly of the earth

We are ransoms in our prisons of fire
But no silent steps can ever pass us

Lioness; see the ears of the forest
Standing for ever erect at your passing

You were the zephyr of the high grass
The grass swayed always at your passing

2

You knew lioness, how power speaks always
Most lethally without blast and horror

Like the very silent voice of fragrant flowers
Like dew on leaves in the early morning

Your heart serrated our prisons of fire
And the nation saw your lightning streak

You tore through the darkness of our sad lives
You quaked the poles of the Union Jack

You touched the spirit of Margaret Ekpo
Who took the baton of the women of Aba

They were rioters and fiery women
With hearts too stolid for Lord Lugard's grave

Hearts with tapers from Harriet Tubman
And the deathless truths from Sojourner Truth

Quiet women who knew men and women
Who stoked foundries for iron bolsters

Bolsters for boundaries bolsters for the nation
And strong new shelters from our prisons of fire

Fires from the great lands christened as colonies
Weakened with brands of cross and swords

3

Elephant countries pound the earth
And there are tremors on all shores

The lioness claims its paws from spirits
And treads the jungles in silent gaits

The cubs owe you, lioness, your silent paws
For the fever of freedom in the sojourners heart

Baking everywhere in the prisons of fire
Close to the hearth or the distant wilderness

Time is silent always and forever
And winners travel along in silent steps

Silent steps like lightning streaks
Are great thunders waiting to confirm

The serrated dark walls of our troubled skies
The noise after the spark of the detonation

The freedom of the air on the face of suffering
Ashes in the wind from our prisons of fire

4

Where are the soldiers who wanted you dead
Their names have tarnished from your acrid sweat

You who knew the silent power of water
Over the naked power of the iron rod

You whose ancestors gave palaces of gold
And you opened its gates for the masses to share

You, lioness, whose name was like your steps
A bristling terror before the seats of evil

A silent joy from the shelter of spirits
Was communion joy for the hearts of warriors

Silently, lioness, you rode the high grass
The wind presses its thumb on all our memories

Silently, the little chicken runs in a dance
With the mystic grace of all chosen souls

The crash always belongs to the angry chaser
Like the flounder and fall of the lumbering beast

The masters' lash outlasts his stolen names
Like the spoor of animals forever in the wind

We who remember Lord Lugard's golden grave
Will remember always the source of the gold . . .

18

Pain

Bose Ademilua-Afolayan

I have known pain
not the deliberate
pinch of restless fingers
turning and turning
in the face of the moon
nor the first meeting
of a new birth
felt at the movement of life
when my loved one moved on.

I have known pain
written in bold letters
on faces of women and children
displaced desolate deprived.

I have seen pain
mirrored in the kiss of Judas
amid fences of men
alone

pain deeper than
you can feel.

My body writhes
in a pool of agony
my face contorted
from its own making.

19

Can You Hook A Brother Up?

John C. Gaston

"Yo, what's go'n on *home*?"
"You got it man. I'm *jest count'n dem days.*"
   "Hey you *remember* that little *dude we used to make fun of in the*
8th grade?"
   "Eight grade? *Yeah; oh yeah; (laughs)* the dude we use to call 'Car-
toon'?"
   "Yeah, that's the one."
   "Man that dude was *pitiful.* We was always *dissing* him.
   We told him he *wasn't Black!*
He *couldn't* play no ball;
didn't drink;
didn't get high;
didn't have no honeys calling him;
went to class all the time,
he even *wore* his pants up *around his waist.*
Wonder *whatever happen to him?"*
   "Man didn't you hear?
I heard he done *made it. Went to college—and graduated!*
He got a *big office downtown—got folks working for him.*"

"*You serious?*"

"Yeah man. And they say he done *opened up some kind of rec center back in the hood*, and started some kind of protection program for old folks."

"That's *deep*. Hey man, *we* need to check that dude out. Maybe when we come up for *parole* he'll *give us a job*.
You think he will 'hook a brother up'?"

20

Dilla

Ronald Dorris

They had begged her not to go. She would hear nothing to the contrary. Her mind was set. After all, wasn't she well protected. Everyone
knew that she had been born with her armor intact. And she was tough.
Her legs were short but sturdy. When she planted her feet firmly on the
ground, she showed the fierceness of her determination to take a bold
stand. The old ones were getting up in age, but were proud that one so
young could move with lightning speed and burrow her way into a hole
where none was visible. She slept throughout the day. That was not unusual. All of her clan did the same. What concerned all who knew and
loved her, through no fault of her own, is that like them her habits were
nocturnal. Yet something about her made them feel she was destined for
brightness; destined for sunshine. The vermin in her environment were
no different from men who feed on fear. If she were to survive, she could
not allow herself to be devoured by them. Instead, she had to feed on
them. It was a cool October night; hog-killing season in Louisiana. In
fact, a hog killing was scheduled for tomorrow.

John Ashcross was in town. He was a reporter, simply passing
through, he said, trying to get a story to return up North to make a name
for himself. He had heard that the South is backward, a region that loves

coon-hunting more than it does dog-racing. Of course, John Ashcross did not say such a thing out loud, otherwise he might have become the hunted. But never mind, he did not need to say such a thing. Everyone saw the sneer in his face. John Ashcross was always stepping where he did not belong, in horse pies, in dog biscuits, and just about everywhere else his shoes tramped. John Ashcross was always cussing when he was stepping where he did not belong. Simply put, John Ashcross did not need to be where he was, which means, John Ashcross did not need to be looking for a story. John Ashcross stepped in mud, John Ashcross cussed. John Ashcross got bit by a mosquito, John Ashcross cussed. A tweetie-bird landed his breakfast on John Ashcross' shoulder, John Ashcross cussed. Everyone was of the same opinion. John Ashcross should have stayed up North. John Ashcross coming down South and poking around could not lead to anything but trouble, everyone cried. John Ashcross needed to go back to the land of cement and skyscraper.

Dilla was on her turf. Unlike some of her relatives who sported six-banded or three-banded coats, her coat was one of nine bands. Simply put, she was striking! Her most pronounced feature was her eyes, captivating in all their intensity in the darkness of night. So when John Ashcross came riding along in the cool of the night in his rental car from up North (still cussing because he was being bitten by mosquitoes) in a split second the first thing he saw and the last thing he saw was her eyes. He had been too preoccupied reeling from the slap to his own neck to massacre the mosquito singing in his ear that he had not had enough time to swerve the car the split second he had looked up. So he had gone crashing straight into her. After that split second he had looked into her eyes, John Ashcross heard a crunch, the sound of a body being crushed and grounded into pavement. And then he heard a screech, the sound of his own life coming to a grinding halt. He had wanted a story, but not like this. What was that?! What had he hit? Those eyes, that is what had blinded him. What were those eyes doing in the middle of the road? He did not want to know. He did not want to find out. He had caused the accident. That was enough. He was in the South. So John Ashcross lifted his foot from the break, placed it on the gas pedal, took off, and never looked back.

Although they had not heard a scream, they had heard the screech. This was something they had always feared, ever since the road had been paved in 1957. They did not stand a chance of burrowing their way into cement in the face of danger. When the road had been only dirt, always they had been able to calculate, based on an encroaching sound, to burrow their way to safety. When they heard the screech, their hearts dropped. This was their worst nightmare. They had hoped against hope that it was not one of their own. But this was their territory, so they had to brave for the worst. With their cry ringing in unison, they raced to the scene. They wasted no time. Immediately, they surrounded her body in a protective circle, and let out one mournful wale in unison before receding to their armadillo enclave in the woods.

21

Queen Etouffée

Ronald Dorris

The old folks say that Queen Etouffée had one major goal in life, to be the best swimmer the world of the bayou had ever known. Despite her shiny coat of red, so many people who visited Louisiana and were unfamiliar with her lot called Queen Etouffée a low down stinking dirty mud bug. Such people had no sense of her passion for living. Such people did not see her crawling her way toward greatness, inching along the marshes to reach the sunlight. She had been one among a nest of many little crumb pickers born to Mem Bisque and Daddy Bisque. Simply they called her Daughter, proud that they had named her Queen so that others might keep her on the throne with positive name calling. The old folks say that her parents had reasoned that if they could add royalty to her mud crawling, her greatness might be assured.

One day an eye-glassed tourist was in a *piroque* along with two others from some skyscraper city up North, being guided through the swamps by One Leg John. The *piroque* skillfully was being maneuvered over the algae. No sooner did they hit a stretch of clear water when the dumb tourist took off his eyeglasses, shirt, and shoes and jumped his stupid tail in the water. When he came up for air, he yelled to the others, "I'm looking for alligators!" One Leg John said if that stupid eye-glass-wearing-up-the-country-tourist didn't beat all, his name wasn't One Leg John. Even though he might have been looking for an alligator, said One Leg John, had he come face to face with one (which could have become a reality for sure in the middle of a bayou in the middle of a swamp in the middle of Louisiana) he would not have liked the looks of the alligator once he faced it, and the alligator certainly would not have liked the intrusion of the tourist, being more in favor of dog than human hide.

One Leg John told the stupid tourist from the skyscraper city up North to get his blind tail back in the *piroque* and put his eyeglasses back on or he would paddle off and leave him in the middle of the swamp. Crawling back into the *piroque* fuming, he did as told, talking about he had paid his money to do as he pleased. Well, no sooner had he attempted to upset the peace of the swamp with his sass, something caused him to jig enough to almost over turn the *piroque*. The eye-glassed tourist from the skyscraper city up North dropped his pants and underwear and saw a tiny little something with a shining red coat and a tail clutching his middle with two paws. It took some effort; no . . . yeah, in fact, there was less effort and more screaming, said One Leg John, before the tourist from the skyscraper city up North finally got the thing to fall to the floor as his comrades helped him to almost turn over the *piroque*, screaming all the while, "A leech! A leech!" Just as One Leg John made an effort to save the little swamp critter, the eye-glassed fool picked up his shoe and sent Queen Etouffée to heaven, when all she had ever wanted was to be the best little crawfish ever to swim in the bayou, but instead met her fate because she had gotten trapped in the funky underwear of an outsider. One Leg John said that was the first and the last time he ever again took anybody wearing eyeglasses into the swamps.

22

Rip Tide

Ronald Dorris

How foolish
The captor to think
Mission complete
Between main land and island
That him a bridge
Could construct
To link Dakar to Gorée
When spirit
Baptized in blood
Secures a protective circle
That strengthens Coumba Castel

They who negate the village
See not construction
Only vision manifest abstract

Do not cry, my Sister
If, as you say,
About this place you have prayed

The last word is yours
For others have not prayed
Nor praised
But have raped without protection
Mindless of virgin conception
And seminal wisdom
Tearing limb for limb
Seed scattered in destruction
Full of cancer from greed
Material in excess of weight
Lest they be considered weak
When energy is spent
Past a fugue in minor key.

23

Will Mamadou Serve as Guide

Ronald Dorris

Only when we cannot create
Do we cry
Self-same tears of defeat
In our impasse to surrender
Baptism and reflection
While we drown in a sea of salt
That stings our wounds
Or turns our trust to stone

To look back
Without the guide
Is to scan
Self-same misery gone mad
Heightened by non-awareness

Why give others delight
To revel in our agony
When we alone master control
To steer the course

Full-speed ahead

Cannot we see
As Grandsire said
We learn life's secrets
Through sacrifice

Our face is not scarred
Those marks are etchings of royalty

Let us not be dismayed
Should we sense loss
Of the ring in our ear
Let the midwife bore
A new hole
As we step through the circle
To kindle power in our soul.

Philosophy

24

Who's Afraid of African Philosophy?

Muyiwa Falaiye

For many years, philosophers in Africa have engaged in the meta-philosophical inquiry on the question: "Is there an African philosophy?" In many such cases, more heat than light has been generated. It is true that some have decided to abandon that question and proceed to tackle substantive issues in African philosophy (Falaiye "African Philosophy" 50), believing that it is futile to deny a people a philosophy, or to assume that African philosophy, and by extension cultural philosophy, must be assessed through Western paradigms.

However, once in a while, one revisits the question, not for the purpose of satisfying the skeptics of the West, but essentially to show the agnostics and the open-minded that every philosopher is a child of her/his environment. No matter what superior logic one is able to muster, it is unlikely that Western skeptics would accept the possibility of an African philosophy, forgetting that two of the biggest attributes of philosophy are its openness and mutability. The following sections will explore the meaning of a philosophy that is African and respond to objections to the subject.

What is African Philosophy?

There are three main ways to determine what is African philosophy. The first is to consider as African philosophy any philosophical system written, propounded, or created by a person of African descent. In other words, once you have an African parentage, the philosophy in which you engage is African philosophy. The second way is to consider a philosophical system written, propounded, or created on the continent of Africa as African philosophy. The third possibility is to consider any philosophical system that deals with what one might call African problems and themes or with some aspects of African culture (Ruch and Anyanwu 5-7). I shall discuss each.

A philosophy proposed or taught by an African is not necessarily African philosophy. If, for example, Jim Unah teaches *Cartesian cogito*, it is not African philosophy simply because Unah is an African. I would, therefore, hold that two Africans seriously debating about *Cartesian cogito* or Hegel's dialectics are no more engaged in African philosophy than two African scientists debating Newton's laws of motion are dealing with African physics.

A philosophy written or taught on the continent of Africa is not necessarily African philosophy. Unfortunately, there remains a great deal of cultural imperialism in many African departments of philosophy. There is, of course, nothing wrong in sharing in the universal wisdom of humankind and in studying the works of geniuses who are recognized worldwide for their contributions to the culture of the universal, as Senghor calls it, but this should not detract from the importance which ought to be attached to restoring and recreating a respectable body of African wisdom and expressing it in a language that is universally intelligible.

A philosophy, which analyzes the African mystery, which concerns itself with the way in which African people of the past and present make sense of their existence, of their destiny, and of the world in which they live, is truly African philosophy. Gabriel Marcel makes a distinction between a problem and a mystery (Ruch and Anyanwu 9). In this sense, color of the skin and place of residence or birth do not have relevance to the question of who is or who is not engaged in African philosophy.

Philosophy can be discussed in the sense Odera Oruka identifies as "simple" as opposed to "unique" (Oruka 45-47). I acknowledge that no subject matter in philosophy is unique to any culture. While it is true that German philosophy is idealism, there are materialists in Germany. While it is also true that British philosophy is empiricist, there are rationalists in Britain. Philosophies are ascribed to nations in the simple sense. It is in this sense that one can speak of African philosophy or any other philosophy.

Standard Objections

Whether in the simple or unique sense, there are scholars everywhere who deny the possibility of an African philosophy. Why? A number of arguments are proposed. I shall discuss each argument fairly.

There is the argument that by proposing an African philosophy, one unconsciously reinforces the position of colonialists, racialists, and ethnographers (like Levy Bruhl), who insist that the African is different from the European, not only in skin color, but also in the capacity to reason. Any reference to African philosophy, therefore, forces a definition of Africa with respect to Europe. They claim that what is accepted as African philosophy is nothing but proverbs and wise sayings, unworthy of the label philosophy.

Another objection to the possibility of an African philosophy is the argument that philosophy in the strict sense of the word, must be a scientific, theoretical, and an individual discipline, just like algebra, physics, or mathematics and, therefore, cannot be replaced by popular beliefs, traditional practices, and a collective and unconscious behavior—what the African logical neo-positivists in Africa call ethno-philosophy. Because, as they see it, philosophy in Africa has not fulfilled these conditions, there cannot be African philosophy in the strict sense of the word.

The third objection is that wherever philosophy arose it was in opposition to the preceding traditions of mythical, dogmatic, and conservative worldviews. They argue that philosophy does not grow out of myths. Western philosophy did not arise out of such. It started only when individual thinkers took a rational distance from prevailing myths. Their conclusion is that African philosophy can only emerge when it is separated from prevailing myths.

Response to the Standard Objections

The immediate response to the objections is that the whole meta-philosophical debate about the existence of African philosophy is largely a Western orchestrated exercise, aimed at demarcating, at all cost, the African civilization from the European civilization. Thus, the European ethnographers have tried to stop the African creative power to produce second order thought and sustain logical debates. African Philosophers were expected to be archivists of their culture or at best, eclectic rather than original thinkers. Regarding the argument that there is no African philosophy (that philosophy is philosophy whether in Africa, Asia, or Europe), my response is that there is not a neutral world philosophy applicable to all cultures at all times and places—every philosophy is a cultural philosophy.

All cultures may observe the same facts (trees, rivers, life and death, good and bad), but the basic assumptions, theories, and standards with which they interpret such facts are different. Differences of cultural philosophy depend on the difference of the basic assumptions and theories about reality. There may be resemblances or similarities between philosophies of different cultures, but these similarities do not mean identity. One needs to examine the basic assumptions of cultures and the methods which the owners of the culture use to arrive at a trustworthy knowledge of what they believe is reality. Philosophers may search for perennial and transcendental knowledge of reality, valid for all people, in all cultures, at all times and places. Nobody possesses that knowledge and history has been the despair of such philosophies and philosophers.

It is true that the African people have changed. This conventional wisdom of the West has no meaning or value. It teaches nothing new. Change is fundamental to reality. This much has been learned from Western philosophy itself. Heraclitus and Marx are two philosophers in the Western tradition who have emphasized the importance of change to human life. Africa is not static and has always been changing. The spirit of creative endeavor remains. The task of a philosopher is to investigate what it is that subsists of ancient beliefs beneath the apparent changes and to identify within the flux of opinions, the great values determined by general beliefs. Both Heraclitus and Zachariah Nyandere agree on this issue (Falaiye "Popular Wisdom" 163).

The opponents of African philosophy also say that Africa is too vast, that the people and cultures are different; therefore, nobody should make sweeping generalizations. It is common knowledge that Africa is vast and that differences of cultural behavior exist. Skepticism of the Western mind can be seen here and the dissolvent faculty of analysis being smuggled into the African cultural world. However, I shall follow this logic to its ultimate conclusion. Yes, Africa is vast. It is true that as political entities, Nigeria is different from Ghana, and Ghana is different from Kenya. Logically, what is applicable to "A" cannot be applicable to "B" since they are different. Within each African country, there are differences between ethnic groups. In the ultimate analysis, there are differences between every individual because of the uniqueness of every individual. However, the fact is that there is no science of the individual. Science wants to know the general case. If the West is consistent with this logic, then one cannot acquire the knowledge of anything, either particular or general.

If the knowledge of African philosophy must arise from the study of every African country, each ethnic group, each village, each household and each individual, then that knowledge cannot be attained. Skepticism arises from the method of science, not from the structure of reality. It is the product of logical reason, doubting its own foundation or questioning its first principle. To spread this skepticism to African cultural experience and reality is completely naive. There are no fields of knowledge called the particular and general respectively. The Western skeptics suppose that a field of knowledge called "general" exists and forbid Africans entry into it. Every judgment embodies both the particular and the general in a single moment. Every judgment is a synthesis of both the particular and the general.

Sometimes one is questioned whether the ideas, principles, assumptions, and theories one presents as African philosophy are those of every African or those of individual philosophers. The people cannot be separated from the interpreters of their culture. If the criterion of philosophy is that every member of that culture should know it, then Western philosophy does not exist! How many individuals in England know about the ideas of Hume, Berkeley, and Locke now called British philosophy? How many Germans know the ideas of Kant? How many Americans know the ideas of Dewey? Why then does the West think that African philosophy should be a matter of unanimous agreement among every individual African? Why do they suppose that African philosophy would arise from their enlightened rationalism? It makes no difference whether a person speaks about the philosophy of an individual African, of a particular ethnic group, a particular nation, or the general systems of African cultural beliefs, no appropriate procedure for the study or knowledge of that philosophy exists because the subject matter has been erroneously formulated.

Some African writers have unintentionally not helped the cause of African philosophy. They claim to have written about African philosophy when, in fact, they merely narrated what their people believe in or do, but fail to teach how their people know what they claim to know. Odera Oruka calls this effort "philosophication." That effort can only amount to "cultural activation" or better still, ethno-philosophy.

One focusing on philosophy cannot easily subscribe to this kind of endeavor, which although it is scholarly, it is not philosophical.

African philosophy is not an argument as to whether the African people have a culture or not. It is not even the description of that culture (i.e. beliefs in God, divinities, ancestors, masks, figurines, tales, and proverbs). Anybody who wants to know about such subjects can consult the anthropologist. African people believe in God, divinities, and ancestors; African people also respect their elders and have elaborate rituals and ceremonies. These do not qualify as African philosophy. African philosophy refers to the fundamental and general principles governing the community of people called Africans. African cultural beliefs, which shape African institutions and behavior, exist whether individuals consciously know them or not. However, philosophy is a conscious discipline. One cannot be unconsciously a philosopher anymore than one can unconsciously be a chemist. Philosophy is a conscious effort to know or justify the general principles governing beliefs and assumptions. Africans are capable of consciously analyzing what they believe and logically arranging them in propositions that are valid and rational. It all depends on what kind of logic to which one alludes. Certainly not Aristotelian logic, which disallows contradictions, but the logic of aesthetics (Anyanwu 34), which says the whole is the real.

Conclusion

The ultimate goal of philosophy is to make meaning of human existence. Since humans are meaning makers, they are not restricted by the bounds of pure thought. What is thought, if it does not influence practice? What again is practice without peace, understanding, and tolerance? African philosophy, and by extension cultural philosophy, will help promote integration and world peace, much more than a priori denial can. One will neither be hurting the world nor scholarship by accepting cultural philosophy. One will only be acknowledging the right of a people to their intellectual heritage and enhance their contribution to human knowledge. One can only promote global harmony by so doing. Who is afraid of that?

Works Cited

Anyanwu, Kenneth. *Atomistic And Holistic Philosophers* California: Heartland Publishers, 1981.

Falaiye, Muyiwa. "African Philosophy: A Conceptual Analytic Approach." *The Nigerian Journal of Philosophy* 15.1-2.

———. "Popular Wisdom vs. Didactic Wisdom: Some Comments on Oruka's Philosophic Sagacity." Ed. Anke Grannes and Kai Kresse. *Sagacious Reasoning.* Frankfurt: Peter Lang Publishers, 1997.

Oruka, Odera. *Sage Philosophy: Indigenous Thinkers and Modern Debate on African Philosophy.* Leiden: E.J. Brill Academic Publishers, 1990.

Ruch, Omi and Kenneth Anyanwu. *African Philosophy* Rome: Catholic Book Agency, 1981.

25

The Science of African Epistemology

Friday Nwankwo Ndubuisi

There is the need to determine and properly understand and appreciate the culture, traditional beliefs, spiritual climate, and religions of a society whose modes of behavior researchers observe in space and time. For example, a thorough study of African religion or art should include an understanding of and appreciation for African theories of knowledge. Ken Anyanwu explains, "without the knowledge of the African mind process and the worldview into which the facts of experience are to be fitted both the African and the European researchers would merely impute emotive appeals to cultural forms and behaviour suggested by some unknown mind" (Anyanwu 77). Also, according to Anyanwu, it is impossible "within the African cultural reality and experience to speak of Art as if it were detached from religion; religion as if it were detached from mythology and speculative thought, speculative thought as if it were detached from mythical feelings and these feelings as if they were detached from moral principles and political ideas" (78). African cultures, philosophy of integration, principles of understanding and of aesthetic continuum differ fundamentally from Western ideas of what consists of knowledge and reality. "Every philosophy is a cultural philosophy, conditioned and limited by culture" (Anyanwu 78).

Even though all cultures may observe the same facts and experience the same emotions, they differ in basic assumptions about, theories of, and interpretations of these facts and experiences. There could be resemblances between certain features of philosophical doctrines but these similarities should not be mistaken to be identical. Every cultural environment and every set of people are unique. This is not the same as saying that a given set of people and their culture are unchanging. As Heraclitus observed, change is inevitable in nature. African societies, just like every other society, are responding to this inevitable law of nature. The people and the environment have always been changing, but this change has to be seen from proper perspectives. "Belief and ideas rise and fall or decay, but the spirit of creative religion remains" (Anyanwu 79). African epistemology is concerned with "the fundamentals and general principles governing the community of people called Africans" (Anyanwu 81). The following discussion focuses on the features of African epistemology.

Karl Popper, a renowned philosopher of science asks, "When should a theory be ranked as scientific? Or is there a criterion for the scientific character or status of a theory?" (Popper 33). Popper adds that while science often errs, "pseudo science may happen to stumble on the truth" (33). To resolve this quagmire, he insists on the need for distinction between science and pseudo science. Pseudo science in this sense could be seen as metaphysics. In its approach to knowledge, the West emphasizes that science is "essentially inductive proceeding, from observation or experiment" (Popper 33). The methodology in science involves the accumulation of facts through empirical and field research. This system is inductive in form; that is the logical movement from particulars to general. Western epistemology creates compartmentalization and a dualistic world. Dualism in the Western culture assumes that subject and object are two separate independent realities. Two incompatible theories of knowledge, rationalism and empiricism, were built on this idea. This led further to the "subjective" and "objective" division of reality. From this dualism arose all other dualisms in the Western philosophy, including mind and matter, freedom and necessity, determinism and indeterminism. In African epistemology, the approach is holistic and nature is recognized as complex. From this theory of knowledge, nature and humans are appreciated as subjects of knowledge; objects are given varied interpretations. In African epistemology, there is no distinction between the "ego" and the "world," "subject" and "object" in a strict sense. In the conflict between the self and the world, African theories of knowledge make the self the center of the world. Every experience and reality is personalized. Every reality must have reference to personal experience. This refers to the totality of humans and their faculties and does not "address itself to reason alone, imagination alone, feeling and intuition alone, but to the totality of a persons faculty" (Anyanwu 87). Truth is lived and felt, not merely thought. "Anyone who wants to talk about African epistemology must concern himself with examining how the African sees or talks about reality" (Uduigwomen 36). Accurate knowledge about a society (including the culture, history, politics, and religions) "will enhance the observed behaviour and give meaning, cohesion and value to isolated facts" (Anyanwu 82). If Africans, for instance, believe in magic, it is because there are certain behaviors and practices that are called magical. The task of any researcher is to unveil the authenticity or otherwise of such belief. "No major advance is possible in science and philosophy or any work of thought if this is made to rest on skepticism, caution, mere observation of facts and the enumeration of isolated facts" (Anyanwu 82). Every culture has reasons and ground for its beliefs. For instance, the beliefs in God, divinities, spirit, ancestor, or the living dead are centered on certain foundations; these beliefs are meaningful and justification is based on human experience. Experience is conditioned by culture. By "culture," I mean the beliefs and ideas that assist human beings to live meaningful lives.

In African theories of knowledge, causation is the interaction of forces of nature, how things emerge out of many interactions, how "one type of force can or cannot produce an effect on the other type of force" (Roy 18). The principle of ontological balance plays a key role in the African ways of thinking and knowing "the inter-relationship among the various categories of forces forming the structure of reality" (Roy 18). Mbiti stresses the need to maintain ontological balance "between God and man, the departed and living" (qtd. in Roy 18). Peace and order in the community is attained only where there is no change in this balance. There is chaos, calamity, and misfortune any time there is imbalance. Roy posits the existence of hierarchy in the categories of forces forming this structure of reality. Each category is endowed with force, but the quantum of force each category has depends on its position in the hierarchy. The forces at the apex of the hierarchy are endowed with intelligence. Thus ". . . divinities, spirits, human beings and certain trees are endowed with intelligent forces and acts" independently (Roy 18). All this shows force is critical and central in African perceptions of reality. Temple explains, "being for the Bantu, is concerned with the category of forces. Force is the reality which exists in everything and in every being in the Universe" (qtd. in Unah 12). Temple emphasizes that force is that reality by reason of which all "beings have something in common so that the definition of this reality may be applied to all existent forms of being" (qtd. in Unah 12). According to Temple, within the framework of Bantu ontology "the all-embracing element which permeates all elements and all forms of being is force" (qtd. in Unah 12). Temple adds that metaphysics for the Bantu consists of knowledge "embracing all the physical or the real" (qtd. in Unah 12). This force is the foundation of reality and experience of metaphysics.

When approaching epistemology, one should recognize the roles played by humans, nature, vital forces, and the interrelationship between all forces in nature. Hamminga points out that "vital power is what matters in life" (1). If there is unity in nature, then it is impracticable to separate self-experience from the experiencing self. Anyanwu explains, "the self vivifies or animates the world so that the soul, spirit or mind of the self is also that of the world. The order of the world and that of the self are identical" (87). What defines humans is the way they are situated in the world, and by the way they act, react or are acted upon by events. African cultures promote coexistence with and the strengthening of vital forces or vital relationships in the cosmos. Everything is infused and energized with life force. This life force pervades and permeates the entire universe, where matter and spirit constitute inseparable reality. This active force has been in existence from the beginning of the world. Since everything is a vital force or share in it, the reasoning in African epistemology is that all things are similar and share the same qualities and nature. Momoh observes, "In African philosophy all that lives is wise" (372). This strengthens the theory of unity. According to Anyanwu,

> The unity of the self and the world, mind and matter is something magical because it defies any rational understanding. We can only say that the self and the world interpenetrate each other in such a way that we do not know where the self begins and the world begins." (91)

The unity in nature implies that there is constant interaction among all life forces. That is why in some instances secret forces intervene in the course of events even those that have been well and consciously planned. This intervention most times is beyond humans' comprehension and conscious understanding. Knowing the laws of nature, expressed in mathematical symbols, may not have solutions to problems. The answers belong to the non-material world. The non-material world is part of the uncertainty in life.

Works Cited

Anyanwu, Kenneth. "The African Worldview and Theory of Knowledge." *African Philosophy*. Eds. Ruch Omi and Kenneth Anyanwu. Rome: Catholic Book Agency, 1981.

Hamminga, Bert. *Epistemology from the African Point of View*. Cultural Research Centre: Jinja, 2004.
http:/mindphiles.come/floor/philes/epistemo/epistemo.htm.

Momoh, Campbell. "Pan Sophism and Ontological Placements in African Philosophy." *The Substance of African Philosophy*. Ed. Campbell Momoh. Auchi, Nigeria: African Philosophy Projects Publications, 1989.

Popper, Karl. *Conjectures and Refutations, the Growth of Scientific Knowledge*. New York: Harper and Row Publishers, 1963.

Roy, Peter. *Philosophical Foundations of Nigerian Traditional Culture*. Ontario, Canada: Sociological Research Centre, 1985.

Uduigwomen, Francis. "The Place of Oral Tradition in African Epistemology." *Footmarks on African Philosophy*. Ed. Francis Uduigwomen. Lagos, Nigeria: Obaroh & Ogbinaka Publishers Limited, 1995.

Unah, Jim. *African Philosophy, Trends and Projections in Six Essays*. Lagos, Nigeria: Concept Publications Limited, 1999.

26

African Traditional Medicine:
The Metaphysical Foundation

Friday Nwankwo Ndubuisi

That Africa is rich in arts and culture is reflected in African languages, music, religions, and sculptures. In the fields of science and technology (though interrupted by slavery and colonial incursion), Africa demonstrates originality and ingenuity, as exemplified in the practice of traditional medicine. According to traditional medicine, there is an ancient cause and foundation for any physical ailment and discomfort one may be experiencing; once this foundation is found and corrected the physical ailment is healed. It is against this background that the metaphysical foundation of African traditional medicine will be examined.

Metaphysics deals with foundations. These foundations are profound principles of life. Principles are those ideas in the human mind which guide daily activities, as well as create harmony between people and things. Once an idea has been certified as the working or guiding principle of the day, it permeates the entire life system of the people in question. Traditional Africans identified *spirit* as the ultimate working principle. The idea of spirit guides and directs all that Africans do, in their traditional mindset. It is then not surprising that the practice of medicine in traditional Africa is spiritual. Africans trace ailments beyond the physical. This explains why African medicine is holistic. Holistic medicine is spiritual, as it is psychological. For healing to be said to be holistic, the totality of a patient's personality (i.e. spirit, intellect, and emotions) must be in complete harmony in tandem with the patient's environment. Therefore, exploring the metaphysical and spiritual nature of African medicine and the detailed understanding of the patient's psychological chemistry is necessary if the traditional healer is to achieve meaningful results. The exploration of the psychological connection to disease is a common practice in all medicine, including that of the West. However, the African approach analyzes psychology primarily from the mystical and spiritual dimensions, while the Western approach treats psychology as an exclusively materialistic and empirical enterprise.

In traditional African belief systems, life is a continuum; even after death, the spirit lingers and interacts with the living, especially those of one's lineage. Makinde points out that "the soul is the thing that gives life to the body. And because its essence is life, the soul does not admit the life's opposite which is death" (Makinde 31). The ancestors died only physically, not spiritually. Thus, they still have power over the living. The name for describing the metaphysical worldview of Africans is known as *spiritual primacism* or the *principle of interpenetrability*. According to this doctrine, reality as a whole is peopled by spirits or vital forces. According to traditional African beliefs, spirit is the life force that animates the world, and these forces exist in hierarchies and influence one another. However, they can never extinguish the life force of the other. For example, the Bantu hold that "being and force are juxtaposed, one can neither decrease nor increase being or force, because being or force is indestructible" (Temple 35). Similarly, Idoniboye states that the "ontology of any distinctively African worldview is replete with spirit" (83). It is that spirit which is the force that determines the character of things and the dynamism that obtains in the universe.

As these beliefs pertain to African traditional medicine, the primary idea is that humans, society, and the universe are all dynamically controlled by the same spirit entity. Therefore, medicine must take cognisance of the fact that humans cannot be healed in isolation of their total environment. A patient's spirit force has to be properly integrated with that of the environment in which she/he lives and the entire universe system before healing can be said to have taken place holistically. This reenforces the point that apart from being the soul animating principle, spirit is the source of unity or harmony in the universe.

Works Cited

Idoniboye, Dagogo E. "The Idea of African Philosophy: The Concept of Spirit in African Metaphysics." *Second Order: An African Journal of Philosophy* (1973).

Makinde, Moses A. "Immortality of the Soul and the Yoruba theory of Seven Heavens." *The Journal of Culture and Ideas* 1.1 (1983).

Popper, Karl. *The Logic of Scientific Discovery.* London: Hutchinson and Company Publishers, 1959.

Temple, Placide. *Bantu Philosophy.* Paris: Presence Africane, 1959.

27

Yoruba Names and Meanings:
A Metaphysical Interpretation

Ayo Fadahunsi

The Yoruba believe that a person's name affects her/his life, dictating the person's fortune in life. This belief is reflected in some Yoruba proverbs, including the following:

> *A so omo ni Sode, Olo s'Ebi, O de,*
> *A so omo ni Sobo, o lo Ajo, o bo;*
> *A wa so omo ni Sorinlo, o lo s'Ajo ko de mo*
> *A nso; tani ko mo pe ile l'omo ti mu oruko anu lo?*
> A child named Sode (Oso has arrived) goes to Ebi and returns, A child named Sobo (Oso has returned) goes on a journey and returns; A child who is named Sorinlo (Oso has walked away) goes on a journey and fails to return, and people start to complain; who is it that does not know that it is from the home that a child has taken a name that inflicts loss? (Adeoye 1-2)

This proverb represents Yoruba names as having metaphysical elements as the proverb has aptly demonstrated the relationship between names and destiny. Thus, the Yoruba believe that it is the name given a child from home that would affect the child through life. The following discussion will explore the connection between an individual's name and her/his destiny.

Yoruba Names

The word "name" in Yoruba is *oruko* which is a derivative of the word *d'aruko* (to mention the name) (Rowland 45). *Oruko* is something by which to remember a person—not a mark, not a branding but a linguistic symbol, a name (Oduyoye 62). Every name/word symbolizes something else outside itself or thus externally refers to something. It is this external import that justified the essence of name and naming.

Among the Yoruba people in Nigeria, an individual's name has great importance. Yoruba names are either declarative like *Ibukunoluwa* (blessing of God); *Oluwapelumi* (God with me); *Oluwatobiloba* (God is the mighty King); or these names could also be circumstantial like *Ekundayo* (weeping becomes joy); *Oluwarantimi-eniyangbagbe* (God remembered me, when men forgot me); or *Abayomi Oluwanioje* (men would have triumphed over me but God disallowed). In some instances, Yoruba names could also be in remembrance of events, occasions, festivals, a loved one, or a deity, including *Orodiran* (the male cult has become a sight to behold); *Ayodeji* (joy has been doubled); *Abiodun* (we have given birth to a festive period); *Eegunijobi* (the ancestors gave birth to all of us); *Orojimi* (the male cult gave me this); *Sangobiyi* (the god of thunder gave birth to this one); *Babatunde* (father has come again); *Iyabo* (mother has returned). Names could also be used to show braveness, affluence and prestige like *Akinwumi* (I desire valiantness); *Adeyemi* (the crown soothes me); *Arowolo* (we have money to use); *Alowonle* (we have money in the house). Some names are also given with expectations to achieve success: *Olawunmi* (I like high status); *Omolaja* (children stop fight); *Olanrewaju* (status is progressing forward). They could also be prophetic, such as *Abiola* (we have given birth to wealth) and *Otedola* (enmity has become wealth).

The Yoruba also have names for those children who they refer to as *Abiku* which means "born to die." Their belief in infant mortality makes them give such names as *Malomo* (do not die again); *Kaku* (do not die); *Kasimaawo* (let us still observe him); *Rotimi* (stay with me). Although a Yoruba adage is *Ile I'anwo, ki a to so omo l'oruko* (we have to observe the surrounding of the home before we give a name to a child), there are some self-evident names which children bear at birth. These are called *Oruko Amutorunwa* (names brought from heaven). These names are reflective of the child's position, the pattern of birth, and the posture of the child's mother during delivery (Ogunbowale 16). Examples of this type of name include *Taiwo* and *Kehinde* for twins.

The Yoruba Concept of Destiny

In traditional Yoruba philosophy, an individual and her/his destiny are two inseparable factors. The Yoruba believe in the concept of *ori* (head) as a vital principle of human destiny. They maintain that whatever happens to a person has been pre-ordained or pre-determined. This belief carries a concept of a supreme being or God (Balogun 74).

Among the Yoruba, a person's destiny is known as *Ipin ori* (the portion or lot), but destiny is sometimes loosely designated as *ori*, which makes *Ipin ori* and *ori* synonymous in popular usage. The concept seems to presuppose that a person's position on Earth, as well as the activities that led or would lead the person to such a position, was already pre-ordained from heaven. Makinde explains,

> What a man is today, he was to be and nothing he did for what he becomes could possibly have been otherwise, whatever takes place, it was, antecedently true that it was going to take place. (58)

Destiny is both a philosophical and religious belief which has the connotation of a pre-destination from a supreme being, God. *Ori* is the word for the "physical head" which is also a symbol of the inner head called the *ori-inu* which is the very essence of personality. According to the Yoruba, *ori* rules, controls, and guides the life and activities of a person (Makinde 58). Wande Abimbola explains that *ori* makes a free choice in Ajala's store house of heads in heaven. Ajala is the skilled potter who makes heads with clay in heaven. In this case, the choice of *ori* is to be regarded as one of free choice since every individual is free to choose any type of *ori* she/he desires (Abimbola 116). The issue of freedom of choice brings about the issue of good or bad *ori*. If a person achieves great success in life, the Yoruba would attribute it to the attainment of a good *ori*, but if a person fails in life the person is believed to have chosen a bad *ori*.

The source of the concept of *ori* and the principle of human destiny belong to traditional Yoruba philosophy. The concept, according to the Yoruba, is conceived as part of God's involvement in human activities on Earth. He is believed to be the determiner of a person's destiny. *Ori* is one of the gods in the Yoruba pantheon; in a sense, *ori* may be regarded as the greatest god of all (Olufemi 69-70). Every person's *ori* is regarded as her/his personal god who is expected to be more interested in her/his personal affairs than the other gods who are regarded as belonging to everybody. As a god, *ori* is worshipped and propitiated by the Yoruba, and this is reflected in some *ese Ifa*, including the following:

> *Won ni k'iyanda o rubo,*
> *K'o si bo ri araa re.*
> Iyanda was asked to perform a sacrifice
> And to propitiate his *ori.* (Abimbola 114)

Metaphysics, Names, and Destiny

The metaphysics of names is connected to the unseen reality of these names. This means that names go beyond the objective physicality they represent. In other words, the names are beyond mere words and sounds, but there is a spiritual link between names and that which is physical. For example, *Mofolorunso* is a name which means "I watch this child with God's help." This shows categorically the helplessness of a human and the supremacy of God. The name implies that it is only with the help of God that the child would survive. Metaphysically, it implies that without the supernatural there cannot be the physical. Thus, the metaphysical causes the physical to exist. A person called *Obafemi*, king loves me, ought to constantly be under close supervision and ought to be showered with a lot of love and care. Because *Ifa* (or *Orunmila*) is the god of wisdom and divination, anybody with the name *Fasuyi*, Ifa produces dignity, should be wise. *Ifa* is the Yoruba divination system. The term *Ifa* is also used to identify the *orisha* (Yoruba deity) *Orunmila* who speaks through the divination. *Orunmila* means "heaven knows salvation."

For a name to be given to a child in Yoruba, there must have been some cause or an event which might have led to the choice of the name. The Yoruba reinforce this belief in the following proverb: *Ile l'anwo k'a to so omo l'oruko* (it is the prevailing situation of the home or the surroundings that influence names given to a child).

The Yoruba belief is that every name is sacred and has metaphysical functions. They maintain that there is an intrinsic connection between a person and her/his effigy or shadow. Such sacred significance illustrates the belief that a person at a distance can be reached by a mere mention of her/his name or through an effigy. This is metaphysically possible; it is a reality beyond mystery and mysticism (Ali 5). According to the Yoruba, *Oruko nii ro omo* (a child's name would affect her/his life and also dictate her/his fortune). In Yoruba, *abiso* (names given to a child) underscore the significance of names. There is a clear relationship between names and destinies.

Works Cited

Abimbola, Wande. *Ifa: An Exposition of Ifa Literary Corpus.* Ibadan: Oxford University Press, 1976.

Adeoye, Caleb L. *Oruko Yoruba,* Ibadan: Oxford University Press, 1972.

Ali, Ade S. "The Philosophical Significance of Names and Meaning in Yoruba Thought." *Knowledge: Magazine of Philosophy* 3.1 (1992): 3-5.

Balogun, Oladele A. *Nigerian Culture and Citizenship Education.* Lagos: Maokus Publishers, 1993.

Hospers, John. *An Introduction to Philosophical Analysis.* London: Routledge and Kegan Paul, 1981.

Lyon, Jayez. *Semantic.* Cambridge University Press, 1977.

Makinde, Moses A. "A Philosophical Analysis of the Yoruba Concepts of Ori and Human Destiny." *International Studies in Philosophy* 17.1 (1985).

Oduyoye, Modupe. *Yoruba Names: Their Structure and their Meanings.* Ibadan: Daystar Press, 1972.

Ogunbowale, Peter O. *Asa Ibile Yoruba.* Ibadan: University Press, 1983.

Olufemi, Morakinyo. "The Yoruba Myth and Mental Health in West Africa." *Journal of Cultures and Ideas* 1.1 (1984).

Rowland, Edwin C. *Teach Yourself Yoruba.* London: English Universities Press, 1969.

Waisman, Friedrich. *The Principle of Linguistic Philosophy.* London: Macmillan Press, 1965.

Wittgenstein, Ludwig. *Philosophical Investigation.* Oxford: Basil Blackwell, 1974.

Index

Contributors

Bose Ademilua-Afolayan is an assistant lecturer in the Department of English at the University of Lagos in Nigeria. She is the author of the book *Studies in African Poetry Volume 1* (2002).

Akachi Adimora-Ezeigbo is Professor of English and former Chair of the English Department at the University of Lagos in Nigeria. She is also a novelist and has published twenty books and fifty academic articles. Her most recent publication is a collection of short stories titled *Fractures & Fragments* (2006). She has won numerous awards, including the Flora Nwapa Prize for Women Writing (2002); ANA/Spectrum Prize and the Zulu Sofola Prize for Creative Writing for her novel *House of Symbols* (2001); and Best Researcher in the Arts and Humanities (2005) at University of Lagos.

Lavinia Africa is a poet, researcher, and member of the African National Congress (ANC). Previously, she taught at the University of the Western Cape in South Africa. She was a researcher on the South African Netherlands Programme for Alternative Development (SANPAD), a sponsored reproductive health project. She has published poems in *Sparks of Resistance, Flames of Change: Black Communities and Activism* and *Network 2000: In the Spirit of the Harlem Renaissance*. She is on the Advisory Panel for the *Langston Hughes Colloquy*. Currently, she is teaching English at a Private Academy in South Korea.

Ronald Dorris is an Endowed Professor of Liberal Arts in African American Studies and English at Xavier University of Louisiana. His poetry and prose have appeared in numerous journals, including *Quarterly West, Western Humanities Review, Langston Hughes Col-*

loquy, The Griot, Genetic Dancers, American Poetry Anthology, Obsidian II, and *Louisiana English Journal*. Dorris is also the author of *Race: Jean Toomer's Swan Song* (1997). He is a member of the Editorial Board of *The Griot: The Journal of African American Studies*, the official publication of the Southern Conference on African American Studies, Inc. (SCAASI).

Prince Mbusi Dube is a printmaker, Education Officer, and curator at the Johannesburg Art Gallery in South Africa. He has worked in a range of outreach, exhibition, and art curriculum development projects. He was selected as a national curator for the South African representation in the 25th Sao Paulo Biennial in March 2002.

Ayo Fadahunsi is Associate Professor of Philosophy at Olabisi Onabbanyo University in Ago–Iwoye, Nigeria. During the academic year 2004-2005, he was a Visiting Associate Professor at the University of Cape Coast in Ghana. He specializes in metaphysics and logic.

Muyiwa Falaiye is Professor of Philosophy at University of Lagos in Nigeria. His publications include the books *African Democracy: Its Problems* (1998), *Africa's Political Stability: Ideas, Values and Questions* (1999), *Perception of African Americans on the Question of Slave Reparations* (2000) and numerous articles in journals. He is the editor of the book *African Spirit and Black Nationalism: A Discourse in African and African American Studies* (2003). He also co-edited (with Sandra M. Grayson) the book *Sparks of Resistance, Flames of Change: Black Communities and Activism* (2005). In addition, Falaiye is on the Editorial Board of *SORAC Journal of African Studies* and *Social Studies/African Studies Series*.

John C. Gaston is Professor of Communication Arts and Dean of the College of the Arts at Valdosta State University. He is also the writer/director/performer of the highly acclaimed play *The Brothers*.

Sandra M. Grayson is Associate Professor of English at University of Wisconsin-Milwaukee. Grayson's numerous publications include the books *Visions of the Third Millennium: Black Science Fiction Novelists Write the Future* (2003) and *Symbolizing the Past: Reading Sankofa, Daughters of the Dust, and Eve's Bayou as Histories* (2000). She also co-edited (with Muyiwa Falaiye) the book *Sparks of Resistance, Flames of Change: Black Communities and Activism* (2005). She is the founder and editor of the internationally recognized journal *Network 2000: In the Spirit of the Harlem Renaissance* and newsletter *Langston Hughes Colloquy*.

James Jennings is Professor of Urban and Environmental Policy and Planning at Tufts University. His latest book is *Race, Neighborhoods, and the Misuse of Social Capital* (2007).

Samuel Ayedime Kafewo is a senior lecturer in the Department of Theatre and Performing Arts at Ahmadu Bello University in Zaria, Nigeria. He is a playwright and theatre director. He has published several articles in international and local journals. He is particularly interested in the representation of women in media and conventional theatre.

Patric Tariq Mellet served in the South African liberation movement during his teenage years in the early 1970s and then spent 15 years in exile working for the African National Congress Department of Publicity and Information. A former Director of Public Relations and Protocol for the first democratic Parliament of South Africa, he went on to become co-founder and Managing Director of *Inyathelo—The South African Institute for Advancement*. His special areas of interest are the history of Cape slavery and African Creole culture.

Alosi J. M. Moloi is Professor of Black Studies and English and Chair of the Black Studies Department at California State University, Long Beach. His numerous publications include the book *The Poetry of Ntsane and Khaketla* and articles in *Reflections: A Journal for the Helping Professions* and *Limi: Bulletin of the University of South Africa.*

Joy Myree-Mainor is an assistant professor in the Department of English at Morgan State University. Her areas of specialization are black women's literature and racial uplift ideology. Her publications include articles in *Network 2000: In the Spirit of the Harlem Renaissance* and *Langston Hughes Colloquy.*

Friday Nwankwo Ndubuisi, a philosopher and a lawyer, is a senior lecturer in the Department of Philosophy at the University of Lagos in Nigeria. He specializes in existentialism (continental philosophy), history as ethics, jurisprudence, and human rights. He is also a Solicitor and Advocate of the Supreme Court of Nigeria. His numerous publications include the following books: *Epistemological Evaluation of Science: The Rationalists Tradition* (2003), *Issues in Jurisprudence and Principles of Human Rights* (2002), *Contextual Issues in Philosophy of Science* (2001), *Man and Freedom* (2000), and *Man and State* (1999). He has also published articles in journals and chapters in books.

Chimalum Nwankwo is Professor of English and Chair of the Department of English at North Carolina A&T State University in Greensboro. His numerous publications include the following collections of poetry: *The Womb in the Heart & Other Poems* (2002); *Voices from Deep Water* (1997); *Toward the Aerial Zone* (1988); *Feet of the Limping Dancers* (1987); and the critical study *Toward the Kingdom of Woman & Man: The Works of Ngugi wa Thiongo* (1992). His awards include the Association of Nigerian Authors Poetry Prize (1988) and the Senior Fulbright Fellowship (2000). His volume of poetry *The Womb in the Heart* won the 2002 Ana-Cadbury Prize. His latest volume of poetry, *Prisons of Fire*, is in press

Patrick Rankhumise, a historian by profession, is currently a senior researcher in the Southern Africa Development Community (SADC) and Southern Africa Desk at the Africa Institute of South Africa (AISA). Rankhumise has published articles on conflict resolution and peace studies.